INSTITUTIONAL ETHNOGRAPHY AS WRITING STUDIES PRACTICE

PERSPECTIVES ON WRITING

Series Editors: Rich Rice, Heather MacNeill Falconer, and J. Michael Rifenburg
Consulting Editor: Susan H. McLeod

The Perspectives on Writing series addresses writing studies in a broad sense. Consistent with the wide ranging approaches characteristic of teaching and scholarship in writing across the curriculum, the series presents works that take divergent perspectives on working as a writer, teaching writing, administering writing programs, and studying writing in its various forms.

The WAC Clearinghouse and University Press of Colorado are collaborating so that these books will be widely available through free digital distribution and low-cost print editions. The publishers and the series editors are committed to the principle that knowledge should freely circulate and have embraced the use of technology to support open access to scholarly work.

Recent Books in the Series

Phoebe Jackson and Christopher Weaver (Eds.), *Rethinking Peer Review: Critical Reflections on a Pedagogical Practice* (2023)

Megan J. Kelly, Heather M. Falconer, Caleb L. González, and Jill Dahlman (Eds.), *Adapting the Past to Reimagine Possible Futures: Celebrating and Critiquing WAC at 50* (2023)

William J. Macauley, Jr. et al. (Eds.), *Threshold Conscripts: Rhetoric and Composition Teaching Assistantships* (2023)

Jennifer Grouling, *Adapting VALUEs: Tracing the Life of a Rubric through Institutional Ethnography* (2022)

Chris M. Anson and Pamela Flash (Eds.), *Writing-Enriched Curricula: Models of Faculty-Driven and Departmental Transformation* (2021)

Asao B. Inoue, *Above the Well: An Antiracist Argument From a Boy of Color* (2021)

Alexandria L. Lockett, Iris D. Ruiz, James Chase Sanchez, and Christopher Carter (Eds.), *Race, Rhetoric, and Research Methods* (2021)

Kristopher M. Lotier, *Postprocess Postmortem* (2021)

Ryan J. Dippre and Talinn Phillips (Eds.), *Approaches to Lifespan Writing Research: Generating an Actionable Coherence* (2020)

Lesley Erin Bartlett, Sandra L. Tarabochia, Andrea R. Olinger, and Margaret J. Marshall (Eds.), *Diverse Approaches to Teaching, Learning, and Writing Across the Curriculum: IWAC at 25* (2020)

Hannah J. Rule, *Situating Writing Processes* (2019)

Asao B. Inoue, *Labor-Based Grading Contracts: Building Equity and Inclusion in the Compassionate Writing Classroom* (2019)

INSTITUTIONAL ETHNOGRAPHY AS WRITING STUDIES PRACTICE

Edited by Michelle LaFrance and Melissa Nicolas

The WAC Clearinghouse
wac.colostate.edu
Fort Collins, Colorado

University Press of Colorado
upcolorado.com
Denver, Colorado

The WAC Clearinghouse, Fort Collins, Colorado 80523

University Press of Colorado, Denver, Colorado 80202

ISBN 978-1-64215-202-9 (PDF) | 978-1-64215-203-6 (ePub) | 978-1-64642-572-3 (pbk.)

DOI 10.37514/PER-B.2023.2029

Produced in the United States of America

Library of Congress Cataloging-in-Publication Data

Names LaFrance, Michelle, editor. Nicolas, Melissa, editor.
Title Institutional ethnography as writing studies practice edited by Michelle LaFrance and Melissa Nicolas.
Description Fort Collins, Colorado The WAC Clearinghouse, [2023] Series Perspectives on writing Includes bibliographical references.
Identifiers LCCN 2023038647 (print) LCCN 2023038648 (ebook) ISBN 9781646425723 (paperback) ISBN 9781642152029 (adobe pdf) ISBN 9781642152036 (epub)
Subjects LCSH Writing centers—Social aspects—United States—Research. Report writing—Study and teaching—Social aspects—United States—Research. English teachers—United States—Attitudes—Research. Tutors and tutoring—United States—Attitudes—Research. School environment—Research—United States. Critical ethnography—United States. Educational anthropology—United States.
Classification LCC PE1404 .I477 2023 (print) LCC PE1404 (ebook) DDC 808.0663—dc23eng20231018
LC record available at https://lccn.loc.gov/2023038647
LC ebook record available at https://lccn.loc.gov/2023038648

Copyeditor: Don Donahue
Designer: Mike Palmquist
Cover Photo: "City Map," by YKh. Shutterstock image 12261706. Licensed.
Series Editors: Rich Rice, Heather MacNeill Falconer, and J. Michael Rifenburg
Consulting Editor: Susan H. McLeod

The WAC Clearinghouse supports teachers of writing across the disciplines. Hosted by Colorado State University, it brings together scholarly journals and book series as well as resources for teachers who use writing in their courses. This book is available in digital formats for free download at wac.colostate.edu.

Founded in 1965, the University Press of Colorado is a nonprofit cooperative publishing enterprise supported, in part, by Adams State University, Colorado State University, Fort Lewis College, Metropolitan State University of Denver, University of Alaska Fairbanks, University of Colorado, University of Denver, University of Northern Colorado, University of Wyoming, Utah State University, and Western Colorado University. For more information, visit upcolorado.com.

Land Acknowledgment. The Colorado State University Land Acknowledgment can be found at landacknowledgment.colostate.edu.

CONTENTS

For Dorothy E. Smith
July 6, 1926 – June 3, 2022

ACKNOWLEDGMENTS

The editors wish to acknowledge the contributors to and reviewers of this collection. Thank you for your work emotional labor, insights, examples, and ideas.

INSTITUTIONAL ETHNOGRAPHY AS WRITING STUDIES PRACTICE

INTRODUCTION.

INQUIRIES INTO OUR WORK WITH INSTITUTIONAL ETHNOGRAPHY

Michelle LaFrance

George Mason University

To understand writing, we need to explore the practices that people engage in to produce texts as well as the ways that writing practices gain their meanings and function as dynamic elements of specific cultural settings.

– Charles Bazerman and Paul Prior,
What Writing Does and How It Does It

[A] "program" or a "campus" for IE is always a site of contest, disorder, divergence, and disagreement—created in the interactive tensions between what are loosely related sets of individual practices that live below official, institutional, or professional discourse.

– LaFrance, M. "An Institutional
Ethnography of Information Literacy Instruction"

Those familiar with IE, will know it as:

> [A] method of inquiry designed to discover how our everyday lives and worlds are embedded in and organized by relations that transcend them, relations coordinating what we do with what others are doing elsewhere and elsewhen. It starts and remains always with individuals and what they are doing in the actual situations of their bodily being, but focuses on how what they do is coordinated beyond local settings. (Griffith and Smith 10).

The methodology has gained the attention of a number of writing studies researchers, who have found its framework and analytic stepping stones keenly attuned to writing studies research undertakings, particularly the coordination of work in writing programs and writing instruction.

Our collection began with our ongoing fascination with writing program research and the study of "the ways that institutions—as sites of everyday work

DOI: https://doi.org/10.37514/PER-B.2023.2029.1.3

practice—organize people and their experiences." We sought to see how others might adopt IE as a methodology keenly attuned to uncovering the often elided, erased, and invisibilized experiences central to the work we carry out in the hierarchical contexts of our home programs, departments, and initiatives. We asked contributors to show us how they have used IE as a tool for thinking about "the situated relations of practice" in the sites where they teach, administer, and study writing and writing instruction.

Work practice, we argue, is a significant entrance point into the relational complexities of our institutional lives. A focus on work practices, in our teaching, writing program leadership, interactions with student writers, and research endeavors, helps researchers to uncover telling micro-moments where the institution takes on a very particular shape, reflective of many complex site-specific tensions. Because IE is interested in how knowing individuals carry out their work in coordination across time and space with others and demonstrating uniquely individualized understandings of the expectations, norms, beliefs and sensibilities most active within a site, an attentive study of work practice, we argue, is one way that writing studies researchers might uncover how powerful and interrelated influences, such as social values, beliefs, norms, professional standards, and/or disciplinary ideals, often implicitly order the hierarchical environments of our interest.

When the IE researcher asks how does our work take shape? we seek to actively re-frame the institutional sites we study as dynamically "co-constituted": Generated when people knowingly negotiate the social, ideological, and material topoi of institutional settings. Who we are, what we do, and how we do it often comes about as we embrace, resist, and recast the prescriptions offered by macro-level forces within the sites we traverse. IE holds that when we attend to what knowing and active people do in the everyday, our research narratives might make visible what is too often implicit, such as the material influence of wide-reaching social forces like neoliberalism and austerity measures—and in this process of bridging micro and macro, we might begin to think more intentionally about how those expectations and ideals have compelled, granted value to, or circumscribed what we do. Once uncovered, these moments often shed light on opportunities for critical reflection, if not intervention and coalition building toward more collaborative resistance, re-evaluation, and re-alignment.

In light of this continuing interest, this collection does not begin where other inquiries into ethnographic research as a methodology or IE more generally have begun—opening with a consideration of the value of one particular practice over others or offering a more extensive introduction to IE as a methodological tool of new interest to writing studies researchers. Readers who would like further investigations into the workings of critical and feminist ethnography or IE, more specifically, will find important initial arguments in previously published sources by the editors of and contributors to this collection.

The chapters we've collected here instead take up and integrate portions of previous conversations about IE, critical ethnography, and the complexities of writing programs, sites of writing, and writing instruction to move beyond and more deeply into these conversations and points of origination. Collectively, we dive more deeply into the study of work and work practices as a means to reveal the undeniable power of material conditions, institutional and field-based values, and the influence of cultures of writing as these shape how people carry out their everyday work. The site-specific snapshots collected here open richer understandings of the cultures of work that are of interest to writing studies researchers, what constitutes work, and how work takes shape within institutional contexts. We offer these new findings to expand exploration of IE as a form that can make important contributions to the fields' many ongoing conversations about the nature of our work, labor, and other writing-related interests.

PRAXIS POINTS: MAKING THE MOVES OF IE

> People participate in social relations, often unknowingly, as they act competently and knowledgeably to concert and coordinate their own actions with professional standards.
>
> – Marie Campbell and Francis Gregor, *Mapping Social Relations: A Primer in Doing Institutional Ethnography*

This highly theoretical backdrop translates into a flexible, dynamic, and scalable set of moves for researchers interested in the study of institutionally organized work practices, processes, and lived experiences, as this section will lay out. While IE research seeks to explore individual experience, it also seeks to give voice to how the micro-moments of those work landscapes take shape—how things happen (in the parlance of IE)—uncovering what practices constitute the institution as we think of it, how discourse may be understood to compel and coordinate those practices, and how norms of practice speak to, for, and over individuals. In the IE framework, the institution is co-created in the "interindividual" interplay between ruling relations and the everyday work of individuals (Smith *Sociology*). Dorothy Smith's framework asks researchers to interrogate their own understandings of a setting as they begin a study, so that those preconceived ideals of organizational standards, forms, and relationships do not erase important understandings of what is actually happening.

IE's focus on the day-to-day work life of individuals and how work is coordinated across time and space, as well as its emphasis on how the practice of those individuals takes shape with/in their institutions, provides a methodology for explicating, and thereby gaining insight into the actualities of our academic work lives. IE sets out a number of key points that are central to its shifts of frame. Some researchers have called these "heuristics"—though Marjorie DeVault has suggested that "ruling relations" are not a heuristic, but instead "an expansive, historically specific apparatus of management and control that arose with the development of corporate capitalism [that] supports its operation" (295)—as they can provide a regularized model of analysis for a study.

For those involved in writing programs or the study or writing, writers, and the sites where writing and writing instruction take shape, these analytic tools are also useful as reflexive moments and gut-checks. We do not offer them as checklists or a series of rote moves, but rather as reflexive opportunities for thinking about the shifts toward the coordination of practice that IE requires. In this collection, these terms are foundational to the studies our authors undertake, so we offer anchoring understandings of these terms and initial gestures towards how those terms are used in specific chapters, allowing our authors to stretch into the ways these key terms helped them structure their studies. The definitions we offer below apply throughout the book.

Experience: Smith writes:

> The term experience is used to refer to what people come to know that originates in people's bodily being and action. Only the experiencer can speak of her or his experience. It emerges for the ethnographer in dialogue, spoken or written, among particular people at particular times and in particular places, including self-reflection. Institutional ethnographers sometimes refer to lived experience to locate those interchanges of awareness, recognition, feeling, noticing, and provide sources for experience as it is evoked in dialog. (*Sociology* 229)

Institutions: Ervin defined institutions as "complex[es] of relationships between discursive and material constructs (124). Porter et al. have subsequently defined institutions as "rhetorically constructed human designs" (123). Michelle LaFrance and Melissa Nicolas defined institutions as "shapeshifters" that are rhetorically and structurally cued to the standpoints of individuals, such that

> [A] professor experiences "university" very differently from the student who experiences "university" very differently from her parents who, again, experience "university" very differently from the trustees. And even an individual's micro-level account of "university" changes over time: a first-year student has a

different relationship with "university" than a senior whose definition will change as she becomes an alumnae. (131)

Drawing from this understanding of institutions as complex sites co-constituted
in the relational and experiential moments of the everyday (LaFrance).

Institutional Discourse: Similar to the broader category of "ideological discourse," institutional discourse operates at meta-levels to rhetorically coordinate
conceptions of, so, what people are expected to do. Institutional discourse creates generalizations which offer a sense of continuity across individuals, practices, times, and sites.

Institutional Circuits: The mechanisms of accountability and authority that
distribute, differentiate, and lend value to particular types of work, "in such a
way that an institutional course of action can follow" (Griffith and Smith 10).
These often take shape around ideals of professionalism, expertise, as they seek
to regulate, or "standardize" what people do, mediating idiosyncrasies and variability in local settings

Ruling Relations: "Ruling relations" have been defined by Smith as "that
extraordinary yet ordinary complex of relations . . . that connect us across space
and time and organize our everyday lives" (*Institutional* 8). Closely tied to concepts like expertise, marginality, influence, and values, ruling relations remind
us that working conditions and daily routines are not accidental, but bear traces
of ideology, history, and social influence. "Social mechanisms grant practices
legitimacy . . . [T]he social order comes to sanction doing, knowing, and being"
(LaFrance and Nicolas 130). Ruling relations carry ideas, language, and rhetorical frameworks between individuals (even those with little personal interaction),
impose ideals of practice and affiliation. As such, ruling relations shape thinking
and doing within institutional settings, routines and conditions are not accidental, but bear traces of ideology, history, and social influence.

Standpoint: This term draws from feminist cultural materialism and feminist
critical theories of the 1970s and 1980s (See Harding) and foregrounds participants and researchers as materially situated within local contexts, unique and
embodied in space/time. The term recognizes that all knowledge is "partial,"
grounded in "material experience," and a reflection of social dynamics.

Texts, Textual Coordination, Boss Texts: Smith writes:

> [T]exts and documents make possible the appearance of the
> same set of words, numbers or images in multiple local sites,
> however differently they may be read and taken up. They pro-
> vide for the standardized recognizability of people's doings as
> organizational or institutional as well as for their coordination
> across multiple local settings and times. ("Texts" 163)

Work: Denotes a series or sequence of coordinated practices within a local setting that an individual routinely puts time and energy into. Institutions coordinate the experiences and practices of individuals through their work. IE researchers might think of work as multilayered, first and foremost a conceptual or ideological coordinating force (think the difference between faculty and staff, for instance, or the differences afforded tenured, tenure line, and contingent faculty); work then takes a secondary and material shape when it surfaces as the telling "micro-moments" where those dynamic and multilayered materialities have shown their influence in how people go about doing what they do.

Writing: All told, in the IE frame, writing, a micro-level action, is inseparable from other macro-level considerations, such as work and labor, or the larger site-specific and social contexts of austerity—as Tony Scott notes, "the distinction is a matter of emphasis and perspective rather than material reality" (9). (We might think of writing instruction similarly.)

We offer these key terms as central to the studies adopted when using IE—some of our contributors took them up as starting points for developing their projects, others saw them as tools for analyzing data sets, or as what to look for when unpacking the highly situated actualities of practice within the programs, sites of writing, and writing instruction they studied. We note that the terms are often difficult to understand in isolation, even as one term used singularly, "Boss Texts" or "Work," for instance, might provide a central focus for an important project within a writing program. IE enters a field already attuned to many of the critical interventions, core questions, and epistemological challenges central to work with ethnography. And, potentially, IE offers us some ways of thinking about how we might undertake the study of work, labor, and writing instruction. In that effort, we turn to the ways ethnographers have helped us to understand the study of writing.

IN THIS COLLECTION

To establish the theoretical assumptions of his collection, we open with a theoretical chapter that traces the ways our key terms—practice, work, and work practices—have been adopted in writing studies research. I argue that "unravel[ing] the histories and assumptions commonly indexed by the use of these terms" is important not only for deepening our work with IE, but for truly embracing its social justice possibilities. This chapter continues conversations begun elsewhere about the value of IE and adaptations to its framework for the study of writing, writers, writing instruction, and sites of writing, but also further research-based conversations about the nature of our work, our experiences as workers within institutional contexts, and how we participate in, if not resist and remake, those sites towards more equity and inclusion.

Responding to the framework sketched in Chapter 1, the remaining chapters in this collection demonstrate what writing studies researchers have uncovered about the many ways institutions coordinate the experiences and practices and, so work, of individuals. Using IE to study the "work" that people carry out uncovers the deep and often hidden investments and experiences of those people, making visible the values, practices, beliefs, and belongings that circulate below more visible or dominant discourses. The researcher might then uncover opportunities for recognition, conversation, or intervention. Because so much about how people carry out their social lives is undergoing radical change in the 21st century—an age where higher ed is clearly coordinated by the material discursive structures of austerity politics (Scott and Welch), those interested in how actual people are negotiating these emerging contexts have found the study of work an invaluable tool for unpacking how our labor in sites of writing takes on value, how literacies and sites of instruction take the shapes that they do, and how we may negotiate each of these interlocking social circuits toward more proactive ends.

Anicca Cox's contribution details her study of how writing program teaching observations are taken up by both the observed and the observer. Her investigation reveals what she calls the "means well paradigm" (MWP), which posits that while writing programs often have positive intentions in their management strategies and professional activities may catalyze important conversations about practice within a program, these activities may also produce punitive and exclusionary experiences that belie the original intent. Cox concludes that: "writing departments and programs can make their positive discourse more actionable by looking *up* power gradients, and in the case of faculty observation for the purposes of professional advancement, by honestly asking: what is this thing for?"

In "Not the Boss of Us: A Study of Two First-Year Writing Program Boss Texts," co-authors Jim Nugent, Reema Barlaskar, Corey Hamilton, Cindy Mooty, Lori Ostergaard, Megan Schoen, and Melissa St. Pierre "fashion a radically alternative account of [their] department's work," challenging previous studies that had "fail[ed] to account for the complex interplay of individual standpoints, ruling relations, and . . . how things actually get accomplished." Investigating the coordinating nature of two possible "boss texts," *The Department of Writing and Rhetoric Faculty Handbook* and *Grizz Writes: A Guide to First-Year Writing at Oakland University* (Schoen), the authors found that their "department's boss texts act, react, and interact with one another in complex ways." "The methods of IE," they noted, enabled them to "appreciate the nuanced and nondeterministic ways that policy texts move from the pages of [their] workaday department documents to coordinate the material and ideological activities of individuals within our institution." These understandings have helped departmental leadership to strategically negotiate a DEIA policy initiative, overcoming tendencies toward "performative, hortatory declarations" that may have short circuited desired changes to the status quo.

Continuing with the theme of uncovering disjunctions and divergences, in "'The tensions in this room!': Negotiation and Resistance in IE Focus Groups," Ruth Book explores the importance of focus groups in IE research for their ability to uncover otherwise untraceable moments of resistance. According to Book, "institutional ethnography provides a way for WPAs to view how instructor resistance is performed and negotiated within the writing program, [. . .] because they show these resistances and negotiations *as they happen*." Throughout the chapter, Book provides examples of the ways individuals in a particular writing program negotiate the tensions within the program even as they are negotiating their own positionality within the focus group.

Ruth Workman, Madeline Crozier, and Peter Vandenberg argue in their chapter, "Writing Standpoint(s): Institution, Discourse, and Method," that writing is both "a vehicle for work processes" and "work in many institutional sites," though many institutional stakeholders do not share this view. Because scholars in writing studies are predisposed to value writing and see it as "continuously coordinated" and "co-accomplished" (qua social), we may not always understand how others in our institutions may then devalue or dismiss the work of teaching writing. The study they undertook provided renewed "exigenc[ies] for revising [their] FYW curriculum to be inclusive of and [to honor diverse] literacies, cultural rhetorics, and rhetorical traditions beyond the 'Aristotelian rhetorical model.'" Such work, they suggest, may inform faculty development efforts and more audience-savvy communication about how writing and so writing instruction might be framed around institutional norms and goals.

Elizabeth Miller takes up the idea of writing as work in her study of the community-based Madison Writing Assistance (MWA) program supported by the University of Wisconsin—Madison's Writing Center. The MWA is based on "'The Wisconsin Idea,' [a] philosophy, tagline, and ruling relation at the University of Wisconsin—Madison" that frames the university "as a land-grant institution committed to public engagement." Miller uses IE to tease out some of the tensions among several boss texts/ruling relations: the Wisconsin Idea, writing center praxis, and the mission of the MWA. She suggests that these texts/theories "fail to account for the complexity of the work on the ground of MWA—potentially limiting both instructors and writers."

"From a Faculty Standpoint: Assessing with IE a Sustainable Commitment to WAC at a Minority-Serving Institution," Cristyn L. Elder's chapter, describes how Elder used the IE framework to explore and uncover the institutional landscape of her university, as she designed and implemented a mixed-methods study about faculty and departmental support for a WAC initiative on campus.

Particularly, Elder relied on IE's key moves to make visible "ideologies about writing [that] might help or hinder the development of sustainable WAC." Elder's study revealed that faculty at her institution not only supported undergraduate WAC across "a wide range of undergraduate programs," in ways that could be built upon sustainably and pedagogically, but also identified "a lack of commitment" from university and state leadership, who oversee "the conditions for faculty teaching and student learning" through university and state policies.

Michelle Miley's chapter, "IE and Pedagogical Possibilities: A Framework for Thirdspace Explorations," juxtaposes the realizations she has gained from working with the concept of "thirdspace" as an additional layer of understanding within the IE framework, particularly helping writing center tutors think through how language, culture, and writing practices meet in sessions. Miley argues that writing center research should be more grounded in student experiences, particularly if we hope to better understand "students often considered 'at-risk' for economic, social, or academic reasons," and that IE and third space provide "a framework through [students and writing tutors] made visible the coordinated activity within their worlds."

The chapters in this collection are illustrative of the ways in which institutional ethnography as a practice can uncover, bring to the fore, and/or provide new insights into the sites of the everyday work of writing studies. They also demonstrate the critical and creative range of problematics, methods, and findings that can be found in studies of writing, writers, and sites of writing undertaken by writing studies researchers. Smith, who passed away in June 2022, as we were moving to complete this collection, would undoubtedly be simultaneously proud and critical of the work we have produced here, pushing us each toward greater discernment, activism, and reflection in our relations as researchers. Smith's influence will long be felt in the ongoing efforts of writing studies researchers to uncover and understand the powerful forces of coordination that order our everyday lives.

CONCLUSION

Ethnography is subversive—it challenges the dominant positivist view of making knowledge. It demands attention to human subjectivity and allows for author-saturated reconstructions and examinations of a world; in fact, it is grounded by definition in phenomenological understandings of knowledge and meaning making. Equally, it is generative and creative because writing research ethnographies are overtly rhetorical; they are producing informed stories and arguments about the world.

—Wendy Bishop, "I-Witnessing in Composition:
Turning Ethnographic Data into Narratives"

We end by foregrounding (once more) Wendy Bishop's belief in the subversive potential of IE and for the study of practice. The urgency and exhaustion of the era of COVID has once more exposed the hard limits of our work as a field. The material and the institutional have been concerns for writing studies for some time, and any number of ethnographic, empirical, and rhetorical methods may be and have been used to study the broader material relations of interest to our field (see for instance, Bishop 1992; Ivanic et al. 2009; Scott 2009; Sheridan 2012; and Welch and Scott 2016, among others). In the span of our careers, we've heard the many calls for the study and revision of policy regarding writing program labor, labor relations, and the terms of our work (particularly in composition and writing program contexts). And yet, we see that for many—in contingent positions, those who live the everyday inequities posed by race, gender, sexuality, and neoliberal/corporate culture—we have clearly not done enough to mobilize, to respond, to listen deeply and with care, or to make sustained change.

We see the subversive potential of work with IE as one means to continue the slow drip of progress toward social justice and equity. Research conclusions, program review, curricular and policy development (and subsequent recommendations), and other research-driven initiatives based on IE methodologies, I argue, are more likely to initiate productive and lasting interventions, lines for further inquiry, and value to researchers when they are grounded in actualities of practice that demonstrate the erasures, the damages, and the violence wrought within institutional contexts.

When we are more attuned to the many different value systems and material realities at work within our sites of study, when we better understand how personal value systems shape classroom, program, and campus practices, we are also more effectively situated to support the people we work most closely with and for. This is a crucial step forward for our study of the relationships between pedagogies and material conditions and for further generating research-driven understandings of how our work with writers, writing instructors, and in sites of writing may claim value, legitimacy, and support in the broader contexts of higher education.

WORKS CITED

Bishop, Wendy. "I-Witnessing in Composition: Turning Ethnographic Data into Narratives." *Rhetoric Review*, vol. 11, no. 1, 1992, pp. 147–58. https://doi.org/10.1080/07350199209388993.

Campbell, Marie, and Francis Gregor. *Mapping Social Relations: A Primer in Doing Institutional Ethnography*. Garamond Press, 2004.

Devault, Marjorie L. "Introduction: What Is Institutional Ethnography?" *Social Problems*, vol. 53, no. 3, 2006, pp. 294–98. https://doi.org/10.1525/sp.2006.53.3.294.

Griffith, Allison, and Dorothy Smith. *Under New Public Management: Institutional Ethnographies of Changing Front-Line Work*. University of Toronto Press, 2014.

Harding, Sandra. "Introduction: Standpoint Theory as a Site of Political, Philosophic, and Scientific Debate." *Feminist Standpoint Theory Reader: Intellectual and Political Controversies*, edited by Sandra Harding. Routledge, 2004, pp. 1–15.

Ivanic, Roz, et al. *Improving Learning in College: Rethinking Literacies across the Curriculum*. Routledge, 2009.

LaFrance, Michelle. "An Institutional Ethnography of Information Literacy: Key Terms, Local Material Contexts, Instructional Practices." *Journal of Writing Program Administration*, vol. 39, no. 2, 2016, pp. 105–22.

LaFrance, Michelle, and Melissa Nicolas. "Institutional Ethnography as Materialist Framework for Writing Program Research and the Faculty-Staff Work Standpoints Project." *College Composition and Communication*, vol. 64, no. 2, 2012, pp. 130–50.

Scott, Tony. *Dangerous Writing: Understanding and Political Economy of Composition*. Utah State UP, 2009.

Sheridan, Mary. "Making Ethnography Our Own: Why and How Writing Studies Must Redefine Core Research Practices." *Writing Studies Research in Practice: Methods and Methodologies*. Southern Illinois UP, 2012, 73–82.

Smith, Dorothy. *Institutional Ethnography: A Sociology for People*. AltaMira Press, 2005.

———. *Institutional Ethnography as Practice*. Rowman & Littlefield, 2006.

———. "Texts and the Ontology of Organizations and Institutions." *Studies in Cultures, Organizations and Societies*, vol. 7, 2001, pp. 159–98. https://doi.org/10.1080/10245280108523557.

Strickland, Donna. *The Managerial Unconscious in the History of Composition Studies*. Southern Illinois UP, 2011.

Takayoshi, Pamela, and Katrina M. Powell. *Practicing Research in Writing Studies: Reflexive and Ethically Responsible Research*. Hampton Press, 2012.

Welch, Nancy, and Tony Scott. *Composition in the Age of Austerity*. Utah State UP, 2016.

PART ONE. ON PRACTICE, WORK, AND WORK PRACTICES

CHAPTER 1.

PRACTICE, WORK, AND FURTHER POSSIBILITIES FOR IE

Michelle LaFrance
George Mason University

It seems fitting for this book series that we open with a chapter-long reflection on the study of work and work *practices*, in order to lend perspective to the use of both terms in writing studies research and for projects adopting institutional ethnography (IE). In light of the weight we place on the key terms "work," "practice," and "work practices" as entrance points into the study of institutional settings, it is crucial to unravel the histories and assumptions commonly indexed by the use of these terms. In doing so, we will not only continue the conversations begun elsewhere about the value of IE and adaptations to its framework for the study of writing, writers, writing instruction, and sites of writing, but also further research-based conversations about the nature of our work, our experiences as workers within institutional contexts, and how we participate in, if not resist and remake, those sites towards more equity.

UNCOVERING PRACTICE

The study of practice—whether we understand "practice" in its most simple definition, as "arrays of activity," or more dynamically as "embodied, materially mediated arrays of human activity centrally organized around shared practical understanding" (Schaztki 2), ranging from "ephemeral doings to stable long-term patterns of activity" (Rouse 499), or as a bridge between what people do and how they do it, such that "bundled activities interw[eave] with ordered constellations of nonhuman entities" (Schatzki 2)—puts people, the power of their individuality, and their choices at the center of our research interests. In the introduction to the collection *The Practice Turn in Contemporary Theory*, social theorist Theodore Schatzki argues that a turn toward "practice" has allowed social scientists to sidestep "the problematic dualisms" that have historically stymied the study of the social order through the 20th century. At the root of these dualistic impasses is a realization that legacies of positivism often focused researchers on seeking pronouncements about the "enduring" social structures that they had encountered (or imagined). This focus resulted in unequal attention to the

DOI: https://doi.org/10.37514/PER-B.2023.2029.2.01

perceived "universal[s]," and/or commonalities across social patterns, and often then occluded or over-generalized resulting understandings of the dynamic, situated, material, and embodied nature of individual experience. A focus on practice, Schatzki notes (underscoring our opening argument), realigns our understanding toward the building-blocks of activity as the doings of individuals within rich and often subtly coercive contexts.

Similarly, when IE researchers begin with "practice" as their entrance point into understanding work, they seek to uncover how individuals do what they do free from pre-limiting preconceptions about what should be going on in a site or what that doing might look like. Within the rarified fields of composition and writing program administration—fields often structured via the dampening influence of what Donna Strickland has called "the managerial unconscious" around writing and writing program administration—this approach to the study of writing programs and sites of writing can be an intervention into the ideals of practice that attend our attachments to disciplinary expertise, dominant models of knowledge construction, highly constrained employment settings, and professional discourses that seek to determine, evaluate, and often norm what people do. Writing studies researchers are enabled to uncover, explore, and reflect upon actualities of practice—what people are actually doing in a site—with more purpose and granularity.

Many ethnographers and writing studies scholars have championed similar processes of "looking up" (Smith *Institutional . . . Sociology*) or "studying up" (Nader), a process of starting from the lived experiences of people whose everyday lives are organized by powerful, but often unrecognized, forces that impose ways of doing, knowing, and being across time and space. An interest in the actual forms practice takes, in our methodological handbook, not only grants meaning to the highly individualized ways people negotiate and carry out their work, but also opens opportunities to trace the how those practices come into being in light of the expectations, values, histories, and ideals of belonging most active within those sites. Researchers might then seek and interrogate those moments when practice takes shape in easy alignment with dominant understandings of a site, but more tellingly how the work people actually do may resist, remake, or revalue those discourses towards quite different ends.

Writing studies researchers have not entirely eschewed defining or theorizing practice, of course. Late 20th century scholars of writing debated the presumed (and often irreconcilable) distinctions between theory and practice at length. Lynn Worsham, John Trimbur, Bruce Horner and others note that this tension in the field arose as a product of the material relations of composition and higher ed labor within English departments, particularly the "stigma" of teaching writing, perceiving writing instruction (and by association teaching writ large) as a remedial service to the institution (Worsham) versus the more vaunted production of scholarship, as theory- or knowledge-making. Worhsam names the resulting "pedagogical imperative," that has often then driven scholarly concerns in writing studies, as "the overriding desire to convert writing theory into classroom practice" (Trimbur 21). The impact of this binary can still be felt two decades into the new century, Kory Ching notes, as "In composition studies, the value or worth of theoretical discourse is often measured by the degree to which it seems relevant to classroom practice" (452).

In the early 21st century, those in writing studies who took up "practice" as a matter of scholarly concern often complicated the theory-praxis binary, recognizing the interreliance of theory and practice for teachers and scholars alike. Cindy Moore and Peggy O'Neill's edited collection, *Practice in Context*, for example, showcased the reflexive nature of "theory-driven teaching" (a term lifted from Hillocks) central to composition studies. Contending that theory and practice are best understood as "blurred" (xi), Moore and O'Neil foregrounded composition pedagogy as both "scholarly conversation carried on among prominent academics in journals and books *and* more of an everyday intuitive endeavor carried out by teachers in their classrooms" (xxii). Through attention to pedagogical practice, they argued, composition scholars might come to understand the "deep structures" (here they borrow from Phelps) of our programs, teaching repertoires, and assumptions about writing and writers. Moore and O'Neil do not explicitly name Paulo Freire's arguments for "praxis" as a genesis for the authors in their collection, but clearly seek to define "reflexive practitioners" of writing instruction, as those who understand the close knit and liberatory connections between practice and theory. "Reflective teaching," they implicitly argue, is always relational, that is "located in the nexus of teacher, student, curriculum, and life" (xi). Throughout their collection, teaching practices are both bound and produced by the disciplinary, social, and material complexities teachers negotiate as they mindfully design their assignments, courses, and interactions with students.

Methodologists, such as Patricia Sullivan and James Porter, took pains to further unpack their understandings of practice in relation to research undertakings within the field. In their germinal text *Opening Spaces: Writing Technologies and Critical Research Practices*, Sullivan and Porter argue for "situationally sensitive approaches to research" (xvi), to account for how computers, as a tool with wide ranging impact, changed writing practice and so our pedagogical approaches to teaching writing. Implicitly their argument foregrounds the power of empirical methods for understanding practice, which they define both as "symbolic action" and as "complex actions that are taken in situ" (9). Their definition of practice moves us more intently into Freirian understandings of the term, as they pose a relationship (akin to the rhetorical triangle) between:

1. ideology, or "assumptions about what human relations should be and about how people should use symbol systems,"
2. practice, that is, "how people actually do constitute their relations through regularized symbolic or discursive activity," and
3. method or "tactics, procedures, heuristics, or tools that people use for inquiry" (10).

Further, in their recognition of the interconnections between practice, ideology, and methods (or tools) we see again that what people do always takes shape in relation to the ephemeral and material conditions that infuse and inform a site. Practice cannot be separated from the unique sensibilities, values, investments, identities, histories, expertise, and predilections of knowing and active individuals. When an "in situ" understanding of practice informs our approach to studying writing, teaching, administration, and knowledge construction, Sullivan and Porter contend that researchers are better able to demonstrate "knowledge as local, as contingent, and as grounded not in universal structures but in local, situated practices" (10). Like Sullivan and Porter, those who adopt IE in order to study practices have argued that critically tracing practice is a move that "views the material practices (of work, especially) as vital to the understanding of social activity . . . [and] Understanding those material conditions is key to changing those conditions" (12).

Those invested in cultural-historical activity theory, also called "practice theory" (Foot), have likewise made connections between what people do and the "neoplatonic realm of rules" (qua theory) that govern writing and its situations, including "communicative norms," such as the rules of language, the organization of the social, and other cultural expectations. Paul Prior et al. write that practice is one product ("an externalization") of people's mediation of environments:

> [A]ctivity is situated in concrete interactions that are simultaneously improvised locally and mediated by historically provided tools and practices. Those tools and practices range from machines, made-objects, semiotic means (e.g., languages, genres, iconographies), and institutions to structured environments, domesticated animals and plants, and, indeed, people themselves. Mediated activity involves externalization (speech, writing, the manipulation and construction of objects and devices) and co-action (with other people, artifacts, and elements of the social-material environment) as well as

internalization (perception, learning). As objects and environments are formed and transformed through human activity, they come to embody the goals and social organization of that activity in the form of affordances for use.

Work with CHAT, enables researchers to see the intricate connections between broader systems of meaning making and the subsequent systematization of what people do and how they do it. The individual and what they do comes to be understood as a complex expression of the social contexts uncovered.

But here we also begin to see the difference between these approaches to practice and work practice that IE brings to focus. IE asks us to start with standpoint—that is, as Smith explains, the experience of "'expert knowers' of their situated work, genuinely listening and watching for their skilled expertise, and learning from them what they know about the smooth running of an everyday work day" (*Institutional . . . Sociology* 8). In this move, Smith draws from feminist cultural materialism, to argue, like Sandra Harding and other feminist critical theorists, against "metonymic epistemologies" that often rhetorically foreclose our methodological undertakings (Harding)—that is, because one site may resemble another, we should not assume that what people do is exactly the same. Finely grained differences may be very telling. (Though Rankin calls for discerning self-awareness in our analysis, as "Institutional discourses can harness the researcher to the ruling relations and impede good analysis" (9).) Smith calls the ways we often miss seeing individuals in our research "institutional capture," (*Institutional . . . Sociology* 225), a series of institutionally-driven blind spots, which are the result of what she names "blob ontology," a false sense of fixity or stability produced by the naming of sites, people and their social roles (56).

Rankin and Smith pose these cautions, because *the blinders and attendant assumptions researchers import into sites often set us up to find what we expect to find:* "[f]or every concept out there, there is taken to be something out there that corresponds to it" Smith surmises (*Institutional . . . Sociology* 56). The goal, then, is to use "practice" as the entrance point to the sites we study to sharpen our processes of uncovering, recognizing, and coming to understand the stories, sensibilities, and affiliations that may be revealed. Indeed, many writing studies researchers have turned to a number of similar methodological strategies to avoid what Haraway once named the "God Trick," a seductive preoccupation with the "arrogant and mistaken belief that we can know objectively, transcendently" (Selfe and Hawisher 36), a tendency that cozens researchers into "miss[ing] the human and very personal face of social, cultural, economic phenomenon that so fundamentally shape the project of education and the nature of institutions, departments, and classrooms" (Selfe and Hawisher 36).

Smith's focus on the individual and the ways identity categories and standpoint may morph dynamically in relation to any number of material and social factors reminds us that social forces may bind us, but that categorizations and differentiations are often more overdetermined and fixed due to conventions in research methods and structures of communication. As Smith writes, "[S]ocial organization is not a concept [best] imposed externally on and used to interpret data; rather, the [goal for ethnographers] is to explicate what is discovered in the process of assembling work knowledges and finding out how they articulate to and coordinate with one another" (*Sociology* 163). The individual, differences (especially within categories), and divergences of practice are often erased by the tendencies of researchers to see systems, patterns, and trends over unique and dynamic individuals.

In light of this history and the interventions that Smith's work offers, we see practice as materially mediated activities that take shape when unique individuals knowingly negotiate their everyday contexts. Drawing from IE, we argue that what individuals do is always coordinated across time and space, understood and taking place in relation to powerful institutional and social forces, but also always uniquely a product of how an individual understands, values, and chooses to produce that practice—a process of co-constituting the institution and its social relations. Practice emerges, then, in a unique relationship to the values and relationships that situate, compel, and organize both ephemeral and more stable patterns of activity. Through these micro-moments, people actively negotiate their belongings within institutional locations, taking up, resisting or refusing, remaking, recasting, and making their understandings of their roles visible.

We argue that the study of work with the IE framework asks us to seek out these uniquely telling micro-moments that are deeply situated with the everyday. As our participants and collaborators share with and reveal to us how they shape their work practices, we may come to more clearly see the interconnections between broader social forces, ideologies, norms, and professional expectations and the many choices, habits, and processes that constitute the institution. Even a small signifier or a minor notation (such as an HR designation, a note on an annual evaluation, or the organization of an observation form) might leverage an undeniable degree of force upon daily life within an institutional context—directing implicitly or explicitly what gets done, how it gets done, and the value that work accrues (LaFrance and Nicolas).

It is this focus on the material actualities of practice, as it grounds the ethnographic researcher in the pragmatic, that has captivated us for the last decade. We see the careful study of practice, specifically work practice, as the means to illuminate those finely grained moments where language, literacy, and so, writing, are inextricable from social contexts, institutional values, and systems of domination.

WORK

Smith's definition of work is characteristically non-hierarchical: "Anything that people do that takes time, effort, and intent" (*Institutional . . . Sociology* 229). Such generosity (if admittedly maddeningly vague) characterizes Smith's career-work developing a "Sociology for People," which began in the early 1970s with her critique of universalist understandings of the social world, which tacitly normalized a "masculinist" baseline, discursively marking anyone who wasn't male (and White and bourgeois) as always already divergent from the norm. Yet, as we join Smith in arguing for research methods that uncover how work practices take shape, believing that these forms of inquiry are essential to understanding how writing programs, writing instruction, and writing itself respond to the neoliberal and global contexts of the early 21st century, we see a real need to look into how "work" operates as a key term in writing studies research, especially those that draw from IE.

The study of work is increasingly pressing in today's higher ed contexts. It goes without saying that Western neoliberal ideologies are inextricable from our ideals of what we do and how we do it—especially as "austerity" politics (Welch and Scott) have continued to stratify our professional identities and investments. Projects informed by IE's frameworks often map these larger sets of relations, offering understandings of consequences, affordances, and other actualities that may not be adequately traced without the tools and strategies offered by this unique methodology. The resulting critical attention to our key terms and their definitions may additionally help us to mindfully reframe our relationships to those we work with and beside. For those who adopt IE, *recognizing others as the knowing experts of their own lives* is crucial. We must not forget the radical potential of that simple act, as it is key to understanding how institutions, systems, and indeed business as usual in a university setting may overwrite, erase, elide, or marginalize vulnerable peoples.

If an interest in "practice" turns the researcher's attention to visible micromoments of individual knowing, doing, and being, the term "work" focuses the researcher on forms, methods, processes, procedures, and principles that are thought to repeat within the site. "Work" also indexes the priorities that lend purpose to what people do and how they do it. Social theorists, such as Devault, argue for instance, that work and work processes are "[o]rganizational strategies . . . [that] highlight and support some kinds of work while leaving other tasks unacknowledged, to be done without recognition, support, or any kind of collective responsibility" (6). As "distinctive relational sequences"—or how work gets done—processes reveal the ways local cooperative efforts respond to and reinscribe broader economies of value (Smith *Institutional . . . Sociology* 54).

23

These moments of process, procedure, and ordering, Smith contends, are where the interplay between individual and ruling relations become visible, as people carry out their work in coordination with the highly structured social complexities of a site. Sites and what people do within them (whether we call this "work" or not) also clearly have characteristics, cultures, shared investments and expectations, economies and/or ecologies of interest to writing studies researchers—indeed, building bridges between what individuals do, how they do it, and the larger socio-cultural contexts of those sites is one of the many aims of work with IE.

"Work" is the character (the "how" or the "shape") that practice takes on, coordinated across time and space with what others do elsewhere and elsewhen. As such, for the IE researcher, "work" can be collapsed into paid labor, but we might also understand it as a characteristic, style, or category of doing, a form of knowing that is mediated, ephemeral, and individualized. Work, more generally, is not then simply what we do, as it emerges in moments of quite personal and individual attachment to doing within hierarchically organized systems of coordination.

Despite the term's ubiquitous appearance in writing studies literature(s), as a key term, "work" proves quite slippery to define, a fact remarked upon when writing studies scholars do attempt to pose definitions. In his "Foreword" to Horner's eponymous *Terms of Work for Composition: A Materialist Critique*, for example, Trimbur notes, "the terminological tangles," and persuasive disagreements that have accompanied use of the term "work" in composition. He writes: "the problem begins with the surplus of meanings that have attached themselves to the nature of work and exert their special pulls," and argues that the confusions are "not so much a sign of muddled thinking as an evasion of the material conditions and social practices of work" (xi). Indeed, these conditions and materialities are quite difficult to unravel. Throughout our literature(s), uses of the term "work" may intersect, engage, and demystify the many tensions between the individual and material systems of social domination and control of most interest to the researcher, but these difficulties may just as quickly be deemed "labor," activity, or some other specialized term fitting the setting or practice, such as "writing," "teaching," or "administering."

In his chapter on "work" (replaced in the updated version of *Terms of Work for Composition, Rewriting Composition: Terms of Exchange* by a chapter named "labor"), Horner opens by noting that his use of the term "work" allows for a crucial focus on the materialities organizing composition as a field:

> For work—demoting simultaneously an activity, the product
> of that activity, and the place of its practice—encourages us to
> think of what we do as located materially and historically: as

material social practice. Further, this identification of composition as work, so understood, also encourages us to think of it in relation to other places, activities, and social forces, responding to and conditioned by them, and shaping them in return. It can accentuate the materiality and historicity of our work, and so enable us better to understand the specific and changing delimitations governing it and its real potentialities. (xvii)

Horner further underlines the three ways theorists have indexed materiality as they have discussed work: materiality may reference the use of tools (such as technology); broader "hosts or socioeconomic conditions contributing the contexts that surround physical production," which connect us to the social sphere; or the "networks" of circulation and access that are produced by "global relations of power" (xvii). Work, for Horner, always indexes the "materiality between students and teachers in the composition classroom," but by this he means the broad ways the social organizes our bodies, being, and doing, such as "relations of race, gender, class, ethnicity, sexual orientation, generation, and region, among others within the classroom and/or in the larger social realm." He notes, as well, the "personal relations (e.g., familial) relations—and the lived experience of history of these relations to which any act of writing may be seen as responding" (xviii). But, more commonly Horner acknowledges, we see work referring to "paid employment," "written texts," and—important for the IE researcher—the "actual concrete activities of teaching" (xviii). For Horner, then, work is a dynamic term, best defined in context, but always hinting, to some degree, at these complexities and layers of socio-cultural materiality.

Embracing exactly the tangles Trimbur laments, Jessica Restaino opens her ethnography, *First Semester: Graduate Students, Teaching Writing, and the Challenges of Middle Ground,* by foregrounding the "interdependence, balance, and, at times, interchangeability" of Hannah Arendt's "three-part theoretical construct of labor, work, and action," in *The Human Condition* (14). Noting that terms like "work" are simply and inevitably "in orbit with" the terms "labor" and "action," Restaino sits with Arendt's distinguishing moves: Arendt compares labor to "tilled soil," which "needs to be labored upon time and again" Laboring is, as such, a sustained practice and never quite finished. "At the end of each day, our labor is wiped away, and we are faced with yet another weedy garden" (14). Arendt's equation of labor to human sustenance, Restaino notes, marks labor as "essential, yet rewarded with the least enduring of gifts" (23). Action, for Arendt, takes on both a daily and public nature and Restaino notes that "Arendt often describes action as a self-disclosure or revelation, where we appear as ourselves before others. For this reason, Arendt connects action to 'plurality' because action is utterly dependent upon the presence of others to witness and remember" (15). And finally, work, which for Arendt is "fabrication," distinguished from labor as it takes on a permanence. As Restaino writes: "the lasting record, made by human hands, of our most striking words and deeds. Work is the product, or proof, of human ingenuity, rebellion, and resistance" (16). For Restaino: Labor is what people do. Work is the material, social, and historical product of that doing. Action—the particular doings of people—takes on shape, force, and meaning around the purpose and permanence of work.

Others, like Asao Inoue who exhaustively theorizes and defines "labor" in *Labor-Based Grading Contracts: Building Equity and Inclusion in the Compassionate Writing Classroom* are more intent on a precise and careful understanding of the subtexts of our chosen language. Inoue's purposeful adoption of "labor," for instance, places us immediately and squarely within the issues of racial embodiment central to his arguments about rethinking grading to allow for linguistic justice:

> Labor requires a body in motion, even if the motions are small or slight. We speak through our bodies . . . Each time we speak, our bodies move in amazingly elaborate and coordinated ways, like a synchronized dance group, each dancer moving their part, forming a larger organism that produces something more than the sum of the individuals dancing . . . When we write, a similar coordinated dance occurs, whether we put pen to paper, or fingers to keyboard, or dictate into a smartphone, our bodies move and our brains work to make and process language. When we read text or make sense of images or symbols, we similarly expend bodily energy . . . When we manipulate a computer keyboard or mouse to scroll through pages on a screen, or lick our fingers to turn a page, our eyes move back and forth, our brains activate neurons . . . These bodily movements, combined with our brain's firing and burning of energy, make the acts of languaging bodily labor, work, energy expended. Bodily labor is fundamental to all learning. No one learns without laboring, without doing in some way, without moving their body. (77–78)

It is the bodily materiality of labor that puts us into relationship with others (and the things around us), Inoue notes.

Inoue's intent is to bring our attention to the ways we value and evaluate what student writers do, the way we value and evaluate language (as) practice(s), and how we undertake these evaluations within undeniable material, socio-political contexts that we have inadvertently historically disavowed, erased, ignored, or too conveniently forgotten as we have—perhaps unconsciously—valued and privileged white language practices over other linguistic forms. We may call these contexts "ecologies" or "economies" (or "political economies," as does Scott 2009), or think of them in cultural terms, as does Inoue when making his case for the pervasiveness of White supremacy as an unmarked form of cultural dominance (the "habitus," he calls it, drawing from Pierre Bordieu. Inoue's work insists that there is no understanding labor—be it faculty, student, paid, or unpaid—without the judgments, expectations, influences, conditions, etc., that structure our cultural systems, not just including, *but particularly via*, education and our classrooms, in White supremacy (79–80).

Ultimately, Inoue additionally suggests that Arendt's distinctions pose labor as a verb and work as a noun (119)—an important realization for ethnographers who sometimes find themselves hoping to name processes, products, sequences, relationships, and tensions that live in between these two poles of signification. And, all of these definitions seem to call up ideals of work as more conceptually or taxonomically-oriented. (Think "career" over "job" and other categorical differences: White collar in distinction from blue collar, educator in distinction from writer.) Put succinctly into context by Pamela Takayoshi and Sullivan, while the meanings of labor as a writing studies concern may "shimmer between" socio-political dimensions the "political" and "assembly line" connections of labor "rob the term [labor] of creativity" and "consequently make it mundane" (3). To labor is to use hands and body toward subsistence; to work is to stay in the realm of ideas and ideals.

To Inoue's differentiation between labor-as-verb and work-as-noun, I add Seth Kahn's distinction of managed labor. Kahn writes, "if we're not talking about how work is managed, we're not talking about labor issues. We're talking about work" (Kahn and Pason 14), a definition that positions both terms in discourses of organized labor and activism. Institutional ethnography similarly reframes labor as doing-in-the world and work as being-in the world. But IE also understands the distinction between doing and being as *permeable*. There is simply no doing without being; this inter-reliance explains why the terms are so easily confused or swapped in for one another in so many academic and non-academic texts and contexts. If labor can be understood as what our bodies and hands actually do and work is what socially shapes and instills value in those doings, being and doing must also be understood as inherently bound to one another. Similarly, those who practice IE, are likely to resist any fixity of the terms, arguing that whether a researcher chooses to use "labor" or instead opts for "work," the terms will take on verb-ness or noun-ness, doing-ness or being-ness, as a demonstration of the contextually responsive nature of the study at hand.

We can understand "work" (in an office, in a classroom, with students), then, simultaneously as a social collaboration—so a construction—and a product of uniquely personal understandings, preferences, identifications, and affiliations within particular institutional settings, disciplinary and professional identities. And in thinking with Trimbur, Horner, Restaino, Inoue, and Takayoshi and Sullivan, we underscore the dynamic, individual, and embodied nature of the micro-moments that capture our attention as researchers, a directed focus we encourage those working with IE to explicitly explore as they seek to uncover multilayered actualities that have for too long been just beyond our gaze.

CODA: FROM DEFINITIONS TO POSSIBILITIES

It is one goal of the IE researcher to sit with exactly these moments of intersection, intractability, and lively, lovely mess, learning from them *as they are* over how we assume or might like them to be. Relations and actualities are rarely as neatly lived as the research narratives we compose. Unpacking definitions can help us to reveal how we may reply on commonplaces, elisions, and assumptions that subtly undermine our efforts at understanding.

A case in point can be found in Carmen Kynard's pointed antiracist critique, "'All I Need Is One Mic': A Black Feminist Community Meditation on the Work, the Job, and the Hustle (& Why So Many of Y'all Confuse This Stuff)." In this talk, delivered at the 2019 Conference on Community Writing, Kynard takes on a common confusion, whereby faculty "base their entire scholarly and professional identity within the college where they work." Yet, she is quick to clarify: "But that's the job, not the work" (19).

"The conflation of the job and the work, however, is only possible for those groups sanctioned within the terms of a default white norm and privilege," she continues. "It is easy to see the job as your work when the people and the culture around you are YOU." Here, Kynard then turns her eye toward the racial erasures and confusions these conflations support, naming them conditions supported by White supremacy and calling us to be more discerning in our understandings of how our work lives take shape through these processes of racialized, ordering, and valuing working bodies:

> The fact of the matter is that Black folk cannot readily find themselves in most university spaces (outside of the HBCUs) and non-profit funding cultures so they have to understand rather quickly where the institution ends, where their own lives and minds begin, and not expect a centering unless by way of tokenism. This is an important praxis for leading intellectual

and activist lives at institutions today because neoliberalism does not love anyone, not even its white citizenry . . . Black faculty, especially those with Black content, know the university doesn't want us, hasn't ever humanized us, and only allowed us entry because of Black student protest. (19)

I would be remiss in my work as an activist scholar myself if I did not also pause to note that Kynard turns her eye to critiquing "critical university studies and neo-marxist managerial critiques in composition-rhetoric studies" for being too inexorably "white."

I imagine Kynard would level a similar critique toward this collection.

And, I acknowledge our need to do better at decentering Whiteness as we take up tools like IE and explore "work" as an institutional construct. Like many tools, IE is constrained by the hands that wield it. And this is exactly why the discerning study of work—our work—matters. These types of parsings and the antiracist work of scholars like Kynard, help us to understand how work that we imagined as liberatory has (perhaps inadvertently) leaned into silence, erasures, and marginalizations of those we work with, despite our intentions to make change or to serve in our roles as administrators, researchers, teachers, and colleagues.

We are called to do more and do better.

I have theorized "our work" in this chapter as a set of practices that are co-constituted in the moments that knowing and unique individuals negotiate their everyday experiences (2012). (In this framing, the term "work" would umbrella or encompass a term like "labor.") Similarly, Michele Miley has argued that understanding our work as always "coordinated" (and/or relational) allows us to see how local frames of meaning allow us to understand the moments people enact professional identities, affiliations, and understandings of their institutional roles. They negotiate those roles through practice.

What we do simply cannot be separated from who we are and the systems of value that grant that work legitimacy. Doing, being, knowing, individual experience, ideals of practice, local materialities, and institutional discourse are mutually constitutive. With these understandings, we might more mindfully carry out our work as researchers, as we continue to extend and deepen the critiques, findings, and understandings that are made possible when we adopt frameworks such as IE.

WORKS CITED

Bazerman, Charles, and Paul Prior. *What Writing Does and How It Does It.* Lawrence Erlbaum Associates, *2003.*

Cox, Anicca, et al. "The Indianapolis Resolution: Responding to 21st Century Exigencies/Political Economies of Composition Labor." *College Composition and Communication*, special issue on *The Political Economies of Composition Studies,* vol. 68, no. 1, 2016, pp. 38–67. http://www.jstor.org/stable/44783526.

Ching, Kory Lawson. "Theory and Its Practice in Composition Studies." *JAC,* vol. 27, no. 3/4, 2007, pp. 445–69.

Devault, Marjorie. "Introduction." *People at Work: Life, Power, and Social Inclusion in the New Economy.* New York UP, 2008.

———. "What is Institutional Ethnography?" *Social Problems,* vol. 53, no. 3, 2006, pp. 294–98. https://doi.org/10.1525/sp.2006.53.3.294.

Freire, Paulo. *Pedagogy of the Oppressed.* Continuum, 2000.

Foot, Kristen A. "Cultural-Historical Activity Theory: Exploring a Theory to Inform Practice and Research." *Journal of Human Behavior in the Social Environment,* vol. 24, no. 3, 2014, pp. 329–34. https://doi.org/10.1080/10911359.2013.831011.

Griffith, Allison, and Dorothy Smith. *Under New Public Management: Institutional Ethnographies of Changing Front-Line Work.* University of Toronto Press, 2014.

Harding, Sandra. "Introduction: Standpoint Theory as a Site of Political, Philosophic, and Scientific Debate." *Feminist Standpoint Theory Reader: Intellectual and Political Controversies,* edited by Sandra Harding. Routledge, 2004, pp. 1–15.

Hillocks, George. *Ways of Thinking, Ways of Teaching.* Teachers College Press, 1999.

Holt, Mara, et al. "Making Emotion Work Visible in Writing Program Administration." *A Way to Move: Rhetorics of Emotion and Composition Studies,* edited by Dale Jacobs and Laura Micciche. Heinemann, 2003, pp. 147–60.

Horner, Bruce. *Rewriting Composition: Terms of Exchange.* Southern Illinois UP, 2016.

———. *Terms of Work for Composition a Materialist Critique.* State University of New York P, 2000.

Inoue, Asao B. *Labor-Based Grading Contracts: Building Equity and Inclusion in the Compassionate Writing Classroom.* The WAC Clearinghouse / UP of Colorado, 2019. https://doi.org/10.37514/PER-B.2022.1824.

Kahn, Seth, and Amy Pason. "What Do We Mean by Academic Labor (in Rhetorical Studies)?" *Rhetoric & Public Affairs,* vol. 24, no. 1, 2021, pp 109–28. *Project MUSE.* https://doi.org/10.14321/rhetpublaffa.24.1-2.0109.

Kynard, Carmen. "All I Need Is One Mic": A Black Feminist Community Meditation on TheWork, the Job, and the Hustle (& Why So Many of Yall Confuse This Stuff)." Community Literacy Journal, vol. 14, no. 2, 2020. pp. 5–24. https://doi.org/10.25148/14.2.009033 .

LaFrance, Michelle. "An Institutional Ethnography of Information Literacy: Key Terms, Local Material Contexts, Instructional Practices." *Journal of Writing Program Administration,* vol. 39, no. 2, 2016, pp. 105–22

LaFrance, Michelle, and Melissa Nicolas. "Institutional Ethnography as Materialist Framework for Writing Program Research and the Faculty-Staff Work Standpoints Project." *College Composition and Communication,* vol. 64, no. 1, 2012, pp. 130–50.

Miley, Michelle. "Looking Up: Mapping Writing Center Work through Institutional Ethnography." *Writing Center Journal,* vol. 36, no. 1, 2017, pp. 103–29.

Moore, Cindy, and Peggy O'Neill. "Introduction." *Practice in Context: Situation the Work of Writing Teachers,* edited by Cindy Moore and Peggy O'Neil. NCTE, 2002, pp. 18–32.

Nader, Louise. "Up the Anthropologist: Perspectives Gained from 'Studying Up,'" *Reinventing Anthropology,* edited by Del Hymes. Random House, 1969, pp. 284–331.

Phelps, Louise Wetherbee. "Telling the Writing Program Its Own Story: A Tenth-Anniversary Speech." *The Writing Program Administrator as Researcher: Inquiry in Action and Reflection,* edited by Shirley Rose and Ed Weiser. Boynton / Cook Heinemann, 1999, pp. 168–84.

Porter, James E., et al. "Institutional Critique: A Rhetorical Methodology for Change." *College Composition and Communication,* vol. 51, no. 4, 2000, pp. 610–42. https://doi.org/10.2307/358914.

Prior, Paul, et al. "Re-situating and Re-mediating the Canons: A Cultural-Historical Remapping of Rhetorical Activity." *Kairos,* vol. 11, no. 3, Summer 2007. https://kairos.technorhetoric.net/11.3/topoi/prior-et-al/core/core.pdf.

Rankin, Janet. "Conducting Analysis in Institutional Ethnography: Guidance and Cautions." *International Journal of Qualitative Methods,* vol. 16, 2017, pp. 1–11. https://doi.org/10.1177/1609406917734472.

Restaino, Jessica. *First Semester: Graduate Students, Teaching Writing, and the Challenges of Middle Ground.* Southern Illinois UP, 2012.

Rose, Mike. *Lives on the Boundary: The Struggles and Achievements of America's Underprepared.* Free Press, 1989.

Rouse, Joseph. "Practice Theory." *Division I Faculty Publications*, Paper 43, 2007, pp 499–540. http://wesscholar.wesleyan.edu/div1facpubs/43.

Rouzie, Albert. "Beyond the Dialectic of Work and Play: A Serio-Ludic Rhetoric for Composition Studies." *JAC,* vol. 20, no. 3, 2000, pp. 627–58.

Sandel, Michael J. *The Tyranny of Merit: What's Become of the Common Good?* Farrar, Straus and Giroux, 2020.

Schaztki, Theodore R. "Introduction: Practice Theory." *The Practice Turn in Contemporary Theory,* edited by Theodore Schatzki et al. Routledge, 2001, pp. 1–14.

Scott, Tony. *Dangerous Writing: Understanding and Political Economy of Composition.* Utah State UP, 2009.

Selfe, Cynthia, and Gail Hawisher. "Exceeding the Bounds of the Interview: Feminism, Mediation, Narrative, and Conversations about Digital Literacy." *Practicing Research in Writing Studies: Reflexive and Ethically Responsible Research,* edited by Pamela Takayoshi and Katrina Powell. Hampton Press, 2012, pp. 36-50.

Smith, Dorothy. *Institutional Ethnography: A Sociology for People.* AltaMira Press, 2005.

———. *Institutional Ethnography as Practice.* Rowman & Littlefield, 2006.

Strickland, Donna. *The Managerial Unconscious in the History of Composition Studies.* Southern Illinois UP, 2011.

Sullivan, Patricia, and Porter, James. "Introducing Critical Research Practices." *Opening Spaces: Writing Technologies and Critical Research Practices*, edited by Patricia Sullivan and James Porter. Ablex Publishing, 1997.

Trimbur, John. "Changing the Question: Should Writing Be Studied?" *Composition Studies,* vol. 31, no. 1, 2003, pp. 15–24.

Welch, Nancy, and Tony Scott. *Composition in the Age of Austerity.* Utah State UP, 2016.

Worsham, Lynn. "On the Rhetoric of Theory in the Discipline of Writing: A Comment and a Proposal." *JAC,* vol. 19, no. 3, 1999, pp. 389–409.

PART TWO. DYNAMIC PRACTICES: ACTUALITIES OF WRITING PROGRAM WORK

CHAPTER 2.

(RE)VIEWING FACULTY OBSERVATION AND EVALUATION BEYOND THE "MEANS WELL" PARADIGM

Anicca Cox

University of New Mexico, Valencia Campus

At the heart of IE research is a desire to create positive changes in the relationships and structures we share with those who we work beside. In writing studies, this impulse encompasses a broad number of activities from teaching and scholarship to administrative and institutional change work. Increasingly, it encompasses a need for deeper collective self-reflection as we adapt to both changing economic conditions, including the disappearance of tenure-stream models, and a renewed exigency for social change in anti-oppressive frameworks. With its grounding in materialist feminisms and feminist standpoint theory, IE presents a useful tool for taking up these concerns in both reflective and actionable ways. IE offers transformative potential in this way because it so easily builds a relationship between critical evaluation and a mapping of locations for positive change. It does so by providing actionable research tools to illuminate shared concerns, identify patterns of oppression, and move institutional participants toward transformation of our social and material conditions. As Michelle LaFrance notes in the introduction to this volume, the way IE studies "practice" "illuminate(s) those finely grained moments where language, literacy, and so, writing, are inextricable from social contexts, institutional values, and systems of domination" (Introduction, this collection).

Specifically, IE works to uncover "problematics" that reveal and help us explore further the persistent conflicts, slippages, and disjunctions in the work that we do, *despite* our best efforts. We do so to avoid "institutional capture" (Smith, *Institutional . . . Sociology*). In fact, those problematics nearly *always* work in contradiction with or "underneath" the dominant discourses of the workplaces we study. Another way to consider it, as Michelle Miley so usefully does in Chapter 7 of this collection, is to use the problematic heuristic to reveal the tensions between the "real and ideal" of our institutional relations. In the site I studied here, an independent writing

DOI: https://doi.org/10.37514/PER-B.2023.2029.2.02

department in a research institution that I'll call the "IWD," I used IE and its heuristic tools (problematics) to better understand the function and impact of course/faculty observation practices. The set of dynamic tensions I uncovered there, the central focus of this chapter, were illustrated by a concept I call the "means well paradigm" (MWP), or, a slippage between the positive discourses used to coordinate work—in this case ones oriented to democratic, participatory, egalitarian notions of care—and the actualities of that work from faculty standpoints.

Exploring the problematic from the "anchor standpoint" (Devault and McCoy) of faculty working off the tenure line, I worked to engage IE's principles of activist methodology by identifying possible locations for change rooted in the margins. In this chapter, I do so by drawing a departmental portrait for context, next, by discussing data from anchor standpoints and administrative perspectives that encapsulate the MWP, and finally, by offering a salient example of institutional change work rooted in those standpoints. As LaFrance notes, "the study of work [particularly the experiences of contingent workers] is increasingly pressing in today's higher ed contexts" and that exigency guided my study (Introduction, this collection).

The findings of this study revealed that those working off the tenure track in the IWD commonly experienced observation and its attendant circuits of evaluation at the interstices of a particular tension in both formative and summative observation. This tension manifested between (1) observation appearing as a sort of "benign" experience without clear markers linking the observation process to pedagogical practice or professional standing, and (2) the ways it appeared (often opaquely) as a tool of advancement. Taken together, most participants were unclear about formative impacts on their teaching *and* about the long-term impacts of observation on their professional trajectories in the department. By "looking up" my findings illuminate the importance of considering shared governance and department design as constellated with observation and evaluation. Doing so uncovered some of the value and impacts of a commonplace practice like course observation from the standpoints of the *subjects* of that practice, an important orientation to help better determine models of shared governance that achieve the democratic, participatory structures the IWD sought to create.

COURSE OBSERVATION COMMONPLACES AND IE

Course observation itself is a salient and standard practice in institutions and writing programs as a feature of coordinated work structures especially in writing programs where we rely heavily on the symbolic value of pedagogy. Observation has been described in disciplinary literature as "usability testing—the usability of [a] program's assumptions about teaching and learning, and also, 'macro-teaching'" (Jackson 45–7).

Observation is relational to program cohesion and the professional development of teachers of writing, and disciplinary literature frames it as such (Dayton; Hult) but it is often ignored as an aspect of the material conditions and collective workings of a department. As Jim Nugent et al. importantly explain, "the material context of writing instruction" is salient to all aspects of how we understand work there as my study sought to do (Chapter 2, this collection).

IE afforded me a more complex view of the role course/faculty observation visits played—beyond professional development and pedagogy—in a departmental space. Here, by using standpoint, IE illuminated what Smith calls "the phenomena of organizations and institutions" in their "nominalized forms of organization, information, communication and the like" that can suppress "the presence of subjects and the local practices." Smith explains that by looking at organizational forms and standpoints alongside ethnographic observation, IE "expands the scope of the ethnographic method" ("Texts" 159–60).

DRAWING A DEPARTMENTAL PORTRAIT

The department whose story I tell here exists within a large, well-funded land grant university. Broadly described, the department is well-funded, and significantly, is not staffed with part-time labor, though its workers are nonetheless, contingent. Its decision-making and governance structures are made to be egalitarian and participatory. The department houses a first year writing program (FYW), an undergraduate major in professional and public writing, and a nationally renowned graduate program. The faculty are comprised of roughly 50 non-tenure-track faculty (NTT), 18 tenure stream faculty (TT), eight "academic specialists" (AS), and around 40 graduate students (TAs).

Observation in the IWD is conducted for graduate students in their first semester as TAs, for NTT faculty in their first semester of teaching, and for any faculty member going up for promotion of any kind. Summative observation particularly appears as a component of evaluation for advancement in an extensive set of departmental bylaws (boss text), a node of social coordination that "hooks" participants into the discourses of the department (LaFrance). However, formative observation is the most frequently conducted form of observation and is not codified by the bylaws. Formative observation applies to TAs and NTT faculty and happens primarily in the FYW program.

When it is summative in nature, observation is connected to advancement for any rank (e.g., when TT, NTT, and AS faculty are seeking promotion). It is not used for summative purposes for TAs. As outlined in the bylaws, for faculty, a "teaching review committee" is formed to conduct multiple observations and write a teaching review letter. TT faculty are required to be present

(Department). Given that TT faculty make up a small portion of the department, this puts an unusually large service burden in their hands. This labor is a major contributing factor to the MWP where faculty *want* to support their colleagues but are overburdened and lack time to do so fully without detriment to their own professional trajectories and well-being.

Holistically, this socially coordinated process extracts broadly distributed labor from several institutional participants who must conduct, review, evaluate, document, and engage in the promotion process from peers, supervisors, and department chairs to deans and provosts. Interview participants tied this social coordination, or "the established ways of doing, knowing, and being co-constituted by people who participate in an established social order" to a culture of care, a feature of the MWP (LaFrance 38). Yet, the lived experiences of observation did not always match the official outlined processes nor the narrative of the MWP. As Erin Workman et al. explain in Chapter 4, "the processes by which . . . work is continuously coordinated and co-accomplished" are not always evident, especially as processes and practices become so routinized as to be "how things are done" (this collection). Instead, here, observation seemed to appear as somewhat flexible, frequently "opaque," and at times unclear in impacts or purpose even within the advancement process.

DEFINING OBSERVATION, EVALUATION, AND THE MWP

Interview participants off the tenure line located slippages in their work around the *value* and *impact* of their professional assessments as they intersected with the trajectories of their work over the long term and as they contrasted with the well-meaning departmental culture which they openly acknowledged they were "lucky" to be a part of.

The MWP then appeared in descriptions of a set of practices meant to support equity and quality in a department that exerted a high level of agency over its own shared governance and interpellated a high degree of participation from its faculty. Yet, the IWD's design was unable to fully attend to persistent structural problems around labor, many arising at the very same locations in which it simultaneously acted as agentive and participatory. IE helped make sense of this, where, according to LaFrance what people do always takes shape in relation to material conditions that surround and inform a site *and* the quite "unique sensibilities, values, investments, identities, histories, expertise, and predilections of knowing and active individuals" (Introduction, this collection).

Interview data revealed this clearly, where those *conducting* observations saw it as useful, pleasurable, and generative and those *receiving* an observation experienced a broader range of more complex associations with the processes, purposes, and practices therein. One example of these complex associations is that even as the boss text of the bylaws outlined how and when observation would be used for promotion and advancement in equitable and disciplinarily grounded modes (ruling relations), participants identified a disconnect between the act of summative assessment and its impact on their work (social coordination). In other words, intentions were clear, impact was not.

Disciplinary literature on the topic also seems to take for granted notions of faculty evaluation as potentially complex but ultimately positive if it is rooted in "best practices" read: formative approaches (Dayton; Hult). IE allowed me to instead seek out the ways observation was implicated in *labor conditions* by building a composite, standpoint-driven view of the everyday work landscape in the IWD, or as Workman et al., describe in Chapter 4, a way to "analyze relationships between individual practices and experiences and the social and institutional forces that continuously reshape, and are reshaped by, those practices" (this collection).

In what follows, I report on a central concept from my findings: how observation was experienced both as a benign act that was required of work in the department and the ways it was understood as a tool of advancement. The findings relate directly to how faculty in the anchor standpoint defined the use, value, and experience of observation as a tool for summative or evaluative purposes.

MAPPING THE USE VALUE OF OBSERVATION

This study began with a 19-question department-wide survey with a 66% participation rate. The survey was used to select 13 interview participants across four departmental ranks: TT (4), NTT (4), AS (3) and TA (2). Three selection criteria were used: participants had been recently observed; were able to identify both a text associated with the observation; and identified a connection between the observation and RPT (renewal, promotion, tenure), or for TAs, advancement of some kind (professionally, pedagogically). Using artifact-based reflective interviews, I asked participants to produce an artifact, preferably a text, related to their observation. Surprisingly, though those willing to participate in an interview identified that texts accompanied their observation, most actually had difficulty locating one for our interview. This could have been in part because no formal reports are filed for observation unless a faculty member is applying for tenure or promotion. Then, a formal letter was filed but it was not shared in its final form with the faculty member.

The most common artifacts shared were observer notes, which participants explained they had to "dig up" to meet my request. For many, this was the only written record they possessed related to the observation. Given that the IWD is highly text-driven, this appeared as a notable disjuncture between its ruling relations and social coordination.

One participant remarked, "well, I had to be observed, that was like, part of the 'gig' (laughs) so I knew that it was coming." But they explained how they felt one observation couldn't say much about their overall teaching. The participant also remarked that the feedback they received wasn't necessarily any that impacted their teaching and noted relying more heavily on peer interaction for improved pedagogy. This turning toward peers is an experienced echoed in the study of Nugent et al., in Chapter 2 of this collection where they examine boss texts and how they are taken up in the everyday lives of participants.

When I asked participants if they could link the observation to their career trajectory in the department, they described that the relationship between the observation and "merit" increase was "indirect" and their voice took on a sarcastic, somewhat confounded tone when they explained their merit letter, "that, by the way, had a single line about my classroom instruction. Right." Articulating the MWP, they expressed that they felt the department *wanted* to build a robust culture of observation but that it would be exceedingly difficult given service burdens. Nonetheless, acknowledging an appointment type that is 90 percent teaching, this lack of feedback appeared troubling for the participant.

In contrast, other participants spoke directly to the role observation played in their promotion work while simultaneously defining it as benign/necessary. One participant said, "My observations have always been good," and went on to describe their experience as, "So, like, so-and-so, and so-and-so, would have to come to the same class and then talk about it and then write about it and then share a report with me. Um, at which point, I am allowed to 'respond' (starts laughing); the whole thing, it just it like, reminds me of some weird religious ritual from the 16th century, it's so bizarre."

The slippages here between the benign nature of observation and its rich, though often unfulfilled potential, were also encapsulated perfectly in moments like this:

> My experience of both the observation and this entire process
> has been that it's rubberstamping. And I am simultaneously
> thankful, that I am, within our department at least, valued
> enough that it's like, yes, just push [them] through, and very
> frustrated that this moment, that is supposed to in some way,
> offer useful feedback is, actually not at all that, but is still all
> the stress of that, right?

As many respondents did, another participant imagined the possible potentials for observation and what kind of tool it could be:

> I guess if I reflected on it, I guess in theory, if I go back and
> look at my syllabus in the fall I could reflect on the ways that it,

> my experience, in this moment created something for me but
> the reality is that I changed my syllabus in the fall based on the
> teaching I did in the classroom . . . it came more out of the act
> of teaching this class than the specifics of the observation.

In sum, observation was positioned by participants as such that it *should* either support their teaching *or* give them feedback on their value at moments of promotion even as they had difficulty mapping how it did either.

REFLECTIVE RESULTS ANALYSIS

I began to first uncover the MWP in interview work. The MWP was outlined consistently in participant accounts as follows: nearly every interview began with a clear acknowledgement of the good intentions of the department itself, a feeling of being fortunate to be employed there, and a naming of the efforts of their colleagues on their behalf. Further, the very language participants used consistently moved into passive language constructions with a "they" or "it" subject use that limited blame or responsibility when talking about negative perceptions of their work. This appeared as an effort to avoid placing undue blame on the department itself. None of the interview participants ascribed negative intentions behind their experiences and all spent a considerable amount of time hedging their negative experiences in the good intentions of their colleagues, and, in some cases, their own participation, in trying to make good on well-meaning acts that they were unable to fulfil. These sense-making moments capture the MWP or the dynamic tensions between discourses/boss texts and actualities of work taking place.

Because IE builds from feminist theory which values and helps us unveil multiple subjectivities, including researcher positionality, this study provided rich opportunities for researcher reflection. In coding, analyzing, and making sense of data, I was consistently surprised by how many of my colleagues struggled to make sense of the tool of observation directly in their work even if they were sometimes better able to define it from an ideological location. For example, one participant clearly saw himself as a scholar of teaching who characterized evaluation as a professional assessment activity grounded in disciplinary ruling relations. He took rich meaning from that work, hence, evaluation was positioned as highly positive for him. But he immediately noted that he went nearly eight years without an observation and so it remained, it seemed, an ideological stance, albeit a well-developed and important one.

In many ways, then, tracking the role observation played in professional advancement in the IWD and how faculty defined that advancement was the most puzzling part of my study even as it was my most central concern. Yet, making sense of this practice with participants was some of the richest conversation I shared with them. These conversations allowed me a deeper understanding of how participants see themselves as positioned in a hierarchy, the roles they play in the department mission and culture, and how they chose to engage or resist the MWP.

Moving beyond just a mapping of the MWP itself to its broader implications as I investigated its nuances, I found that despite a value being placed on high levels of transparency and intention, some NTT participants also linked observation to the "stealth requirements" or what we might call the *hidden curriculum* of advancement in the department. They explained that being visible, participating in extra activities and so forth *might*, they hoped, give them access to other opportunities in the department outside of their appointment types and that perhaps, being observed by a WPA and doing well in the observation would increase confidence in their work and open some of those doors to them. This ran counter to how the MWP instantiated narratives of transparent and linear advancement. Administrative interviews confirmed the hunch that teachers might be asked to conduct a professional development activity for others, based on their classroom teaching during observation, thereby increasing their visibility, an important feature of work off the tenure line.

Another salient concern related to boss texts/ruling relations/social coordination emerged as well. Specifically, the IWD has a well-developed and extensive set of bylaws that guide practice in agentive, egalitarian ways, yet several participants noted opacity around the boss texts they were expected to rely on to understand their promotion process and the actualities they experienced in their work. This tension arose around whether or not official processes, even if they were articulated, were followed consistently. One respondent characterized their experience this way:

> I don't know what to make of my observation experience here. I was observed for reappointment. And, it was very, um, ad hoc. So, our bylaws say one thing, and, what happens actually in practice was a whole other, both times. The bylaws weren't followed for either one of my observations. And so that has always been concerning to me, and I often reflect on, how, it didn't make me feel insecure, but it also didn't give me a lot of confidence in the process in general.

Following the institutional circuitry of observation further, observation for advancement is accompanied by a formal letter. Yet, the faculty member does not possess the letter and so, many were uncertain of the role those letters played in their advancement or even if they were read.

These divergences speak to IE's notion of ruling relations where they:

> Coordinate what people know about what is happening—even if that knowledge does not quite match what is known from being there. Often vested in people's work with texts, ruling relations are activities of governing that depend on selecting, categorizing, and/or objectifying aspects of the social world in order to develop facts and knowledge upon which to base decisions. (Rankin "Conducting . . . Analytic" 3)

Given the ostensibly rich culture of best practices around observation in the department, guided as it is by formative, reflexive, goal-driven, teacher-centered, pedagogical and research-based principles—both administrative interviews and department documents point to it being that—it was curious that again and again, the desire for more summative feedback, in *both* the summative and formative moments of observation, was something that those *being* observed seemed to yearn for. As Nugent et al. explain as we emerge "with a fuller understanding how ruling relations are potentiated and come to coordinate our activity, we come to recognize that the official adoption of a policy" (in this case course observation practice) "marks a midpoint in a complex social process of uptake and activation, not its end" (Chapter 4, this collection).

Collectively, these understandings presented a picture of the social coordination and ruling relations of the department occurring beneath the positive discourses of the IWD and its MWP that were very much tied to the standpoints of the participants located in their departmental ranks with all the complexity and tension they encountered in their work over time.

ADMINISTRATIVE NARRATIVES OF SERVICE AND PLEASURE

Arguably, the positive narratives of and investment in the MWP resided with those *conducting* observation work; it seemed to be most meaningful for them. Those performing observation noted an opportunity to offer feedback (guided by the teacher) and to learn from the good teaching of their colleagues. Each expressed a great amount of enjoyment in the process and saw it as a pleasurable part of their jobs. Each were able to articulate research-based, disciplinarily, and programmatically grounded approaches to best practices (formative approaches) aimed at supporting their colleagues. Their responses captured both the local instantiations of the MWP and larger ruling relations of research guided practice, service, and equity in the discipline. For example, one identified that its use as a formative tool emerges from and demonstrates the community-oriented approach to both observation and evaluation in the IWD.

However the MWP, as it appears here, deserves some troubling; the bulk of any summative course observation in the department is done in service of a promotion via a letter in service of career advancement, yet those performing observations were focused primarily on the best practices associated with formative assessment. When composing a summative letter, they focused on how to "dress" a formative evaluation in a summative text like teaching letters. Again, this contrasts with the desire on the part of the observed for a more summative and feedback rich experience, viewing it as one of the few opportunities to receive that kind of attention to their teaching.

I interviewed four faculty members responsible for conducting faculty observation as a part of their administrative work. Two were TT WPAs, one a NTT WPA and one an AS program director. Interview data showed that those conducting observations saw the purpose of their observation work as: (1) to support teachers (macro-teaching), (2) a way to understand the composite teaching practices happening in their programs (assessment), (3) a tool to develop professional development activities based in shared teaching challenges (program design), and (4) supporting promotion for a colleague (service). Some definitional moments from those conducting observation which aligned to the MWP here included, "It [is] formative and casual and we don't only stay on the subject of their teaching; one of the delights for me is that, with a new starting NTT person, maybe we'll just say, maybe you could try this." Another said, "it's almost like an artifact interview using the scene of teaching experience as a method and a methodology because the idea is always to figure out, what should the learning moment be here?" Working as the primary administrator of the program, another respondent said, "We have spent time trying to think about a culture of assessment . . . what is it really intended to do? And observation is an instance of that." These responses connect to the grounded portion of the MWP that builds the social coordination of observation in the department and reflects how it is taken up in the everyday work of those faculty *conducting* observations. Namely, they expressed care, were thoughtful in their work, and meant it to support colleagues in both their teaching and advancement.

CONCLUSION

I return here to two related questions that drove this portion of my study: first, how does the tool of observation get "taken up" in faculty work trajectories in the IWD? Second, how are those choices and experiences tied to standpoint, in this case, rank or appointment type? The answers to those questions build an argument about the MWP in and beyond the IWD: writing departments and programs can make their positive discourse more actionable by looking *up* power gradients, and in the case of faculty observation for the purposes of professional advancement, by honestly asking: what is this thing for? That definitional work is fruitful. In the case of the IWD, observation and evaluation were held by the MWP and contained genuine signifiers of care, reliant on notions of formative assessment. Ultimately those practices failed to achieve the well-meaning ideals of departmental design and practice for the *subjects* of those practices. The impacts of the MWP over time then, were marked by NTT interview participants as contributing to a misalignment of evaluation to the actual work they were hired to do in ways that made that work invisible and left them feeling unsure of long-term stability in a department in which most intend to remain permanently.

Simple as that sounds, however, it is important to know that IE, even as it seeks a clear understanding of tensions and identifies locations for change, also brings a relational awareness that so often those who you study, *are* you, *are* your context. This relational truth—as we seek to understand the everyday nature of work—directs us to a particular orientation in our inquiries. It requires that even as we uncover dynamic tensions, we strive to "see" generously from the standpoints of those who we engage. Put simply, critique is easy; building something better is the real work. To do so, IE resists easy notions of culpability and blame, of overarching, top-down characterizations of the activities we are immersed in in our institutional workplaces as so beautifully explicated by Miley's exploration of the problem vs. problematic (this collection). Instead, it sees agency as distributed and collectively determined as it seeks change. This interventionist aspect of IE can shift institutional doings at a fundamental and profound level.

Accordingly, I would like to end here with a return to a notion of IE as aimed at enacting positive changes in relational and structural systems of work and a narrative to accompany that notion. Over the course of the year of this study, one participant I spoke with had begun to work on a college-level task force in collaboration with the dean's office. The task force was specifically meant to address renewal and promotion of NTT faculty and was grounded in a single question, not unlike IEs problematic heuristic: *why are all models for promotion and evaluation based in the tenure-stream protocols, purposes, and practices?* Together, they had begun to draft new guidelines for evaluation and promotion of NTT faculty by reimagining a wider range of activities for appointment type structures relying in "intellectual leadership" (Frietzche et al.) over the strict delineations of rank: "The promotion criteria used by xxxx and its affiliated units may be in the areas of teaching, research/creative activity, and/or service/

outreach corresponding to the relevant position workload percentages" (Guidelines). That work later appeared in a lengthy departmental report and as a part of longer term set of changes there that will encompass racial equity, curriculum, hiring, and labor. Their work will hopefully also begin to reshape observation, evaluation, and shared governance. Further, that collaboration represents the complexity of how we can *look up* to better change our shared conditions of work and the agency available when we do so. Such an approach doesn't merely see past or refute the MWP, but rather, *makes good on it.*

WORKS CITED

Dayton, Amy E., editor. *Assessing the Teaching of Writing: Twenty-first Century Trends and Technologies.* Utah State UP, 2015.

Department of Writing, Rhetoric and American Cultures. *Department Bylaws.* Michigan State University, 2017. https://wrac.msu.edu/wp-content/uploads/sites/29/2022/12/WRAC-BYLAWS-12-20-22.pdf.

Devault, Marjorie L., and McCoy, Liza. "Institutional Ethnography: Using Interviews to Investigate Ruling Relations." *Handbook of Interview Research: Context and Methods,* edited by James A. Holstein and Jaber F. Gubrium, Sage, 2001, pp. 751–76.

Frietzche, Sonja, et al. Values, Activities and Outcomes of Intellectual Leadership. *Humanities Commons,* 2017. https://doi.org/10.17613/y9cb-6b22.

Guidelines for Promotion of Fixed Term System Faculty from Assistant to Associate Professor or from Associate Professor to Professor. *College of Arts and Letters, Michigan State University,* 2020.

Hult, Christine A., editor. *Evaluating Teachers of Writing.* NCTE, 1994.

Jackson, Brian. "Watching Other People Teach: The Challenge of Classroom Observations." *Assessing the Teaching of Writing: Twenty-first Century Trends and Technologies,* edited by Amy E. Dayton, Utah State UP, 2015, pp 45–61.

LaFrance, Michelle. *Institutional Ethnography: A Theory of Practice for Writing Studies Researchers.* Utah State UP, 2019.

Rankin, Janet. "Conducting Analysis in Institutional Ethnography: Analytical Work Prior to Commencing Data Collection." *International Journal of Qualitative Methods,* vol. 16, no. 1, 2017, pp. 1–9, https://doi.org/10.1177/1609406917734484.

———. "Conducting Analysis in Institutional Ethnography: Guidance and Cautions." *International Journal of Qualitative Methods,* vol. 16, no. 1, 2017, pp. 1–11, https://doi.org/10.1177/1609406917734472.

Smith, Dorothy E. *Institutional Ethnography: A Sociology for People.* AltaMira Press, 2005.

———. "Texts and the Ontology of Organizations and Institutions." *Studies in Cultures, Organizations and Societies,* vol. 7, 2001, pp. 159–88.

CHAPTER 3.

"NOT THE BOSS OF US": A STUDY OF TWO FIRST-YEAR WRITING PROGRAM BOSS TEXTS

Jim Nugent, Reema Barlaskar, Corey Hamilton, Cindy Mooty, Lori Ostergaard, Megan Schoen
Oakland University

Melissa St. Pierre
Rochester College

We sometimes joke that Oakland University's Department of Writing and Rhetoric must be the most written-about writing department in the United States. Our institutional home is the focus of a sizable number of scholarly works including program profiles, retrospectives, administrative and pedagogical scholarship, commentary, and more (see Allan et al.; Andersen; Chong and Nugent; Driscoll and Kitchens; Giberson et al.; Kraemer et al.; Ostergaard and Allan; Ostergaard et al.; Ostergaard and Giberson; Schoen et al.; Schoen and Ostergaard; Walwema and Driscoll). The depths of our department have seemingly been well-plumbed by this self-introspective body of literature. But in another, more transformational sense, we really haven't even begun to fathom them: as Michelle LaFrance notes in *Institutional Ethnography: A Theory of Practice for Writing Studies Researchers*, our field is often preoccupied "with narratives of program design, curriculum development, and management discourses that tend to standardize, generalize, and even erase the identities, expertise and labor contributed by diverse participants" (20). Looking over them again now, we admit that the scholarly works emerging from and about our department exhibit the same set of preoccupations, as most of them have been drawn from the top-down standpoint that LaFrance characterizes. These works offer mostly accounts of our bureaucratic structuring, institutional arcana, and macro-level considerations of pedagogy while generally failing to account for the complex interplay of individual standpoints, ruling relations, and texts that account for how things actually get accomplished in our department.

In this chapter, we turn to the methods of institutional ethnography (IE) to fashion a radically alternative account of our department's work. IE, as informed

DOI: https://doi.org/10.37514/PER-B.2023.2029.2.03

by the scholarship of Dorothy Smith (*Institutional Ethnography as Practice*; *Institutional Ethnography: A Sociology for People*; "Texts") and as articulated most cogently by Michelle LaFrance and Melissa Nicolas, compels us "to uncover *how things happen*—bringing to light the experiences and practices that constitute the institution" and focusing "on the everyday work life of individuals, tracing work process and textual mediations as these reveal the interplay among the individual, the material, and the ideological" (LaFrance 22–23). By shifting our ethnographic "gaze from the 'site' (the writing center, the classroom, the writing program) to the ways people in or at a site co-create the very space under investigation" (LaFrance and Nicolas 131), IE is capable of providing deeper, more nuanced understandings of how work is actually achieved in our institutional context.

In this study, we examine our faculty's engagement with two of our department's primary "boss texts" (Griffith and Smith 12): our faculty handbook and our first-year writing guide. We present a textual analysis of both texts, and we discuss the results of a parallel survey of faculty we undertook to assess the role of boss texts in coordinating the work of our department. As we find—contra the tidy depiction of administrative processes offered by our earlier program profiles, retrospectives, and other top-down analyses—our boss texts serve to coordinate social activity in a surprisingly nuanced "interplay among the individual, the material, and the ideological" within our department (LaFrance 40). Additionally, by composing this chapter as a collaboration among full- and part-time faculty and administrators, we also seek to create a potentially generative program analysis that accounts for a wider array of institutional and individual standpoints. Together, we hope to not only make "visible the interindividual and rhetorical construction of the institution" (LaFrance and Nicolas 144) but to also demonstrate the unique insights and affordances of institutional ethnography as a method.

To be sure, IE as a method can have instrumental and strategic value for program administrators by offering more compelling models of how social activity is coordinated in institutions and providing "actionable intelligence" that can strategically guide program administration. But more important, we believe, are the liberatory ends that IE can support. In asking administrators to "look up" from where they stand, we believe that IE provides us with a framework for keeping our institutions engaged and ethically grounded within shared communities of practice.

While the kind of institutional knowing that IE enables may be of considerable use in upholding the organizational *status quo*, we believe it can also help program administrators recognize where institutional change and resistance are possible. For instance, as of this writing our department is poised to roll out and implement new policies regarding diversity, equity, inclusion, and anti-oppression

(DEIA). By understanding the complex ways that the two, relatively prosaic "boss texts" of our faculty handbook and our first-year writing guide coordinate the everyday work of our department, we may be able to avoid facile or superficial approaches to this important project. By coming to understand how all manner of texts are mediated by a complex process of activation by individual agents within our department—including important statements of communal value and identification such as our DEIA policy—we can help our policies to find their way into those few spaces that remain unthwarted by the institutional *status quo* and where some measure of progressive change is possible.

INSTITUTIONAL ETHNOGRAPHY: DISRUPTING OUR VIEW FROM ABOVE

Oakland University (OU) is a state university located just north of Detroit and home to over 15,000 undergraduate students. OU's writing and rhetoric department was founded as an independent academic unit in 2008, the same year it inaugurated its major in writing and rhetoric. The following decade brought a number of new faculty hires and a considerable amount of program building. To create new institutional structures from whole cloth required a great deal of intellectual work and that work in turn inspired the flurry of self-introspective scholarship cited above. Much of that scholarship is in the form of program profiles—an inherently administration-centric genre. For instance, the 2015 volume *Writing Majors: Eighteen Program Profiles* was co-edited by three of our faculty members, and it declares "How do we do this?" as its central animating question (Giberson et al. 2). As noted in its introduction, the collection was intended to answer "demand from the field for administrative insight, benchmark information, and inspiration for new curricular configurations for writing major programs" (Nugent 2–3). To be sure, program profiles and other "top-down" research genres can be crucial for developing a collective, macro-level understanding of the work of our discipline. However, we find ourselves increasingly concerned about how those genres may serve to exclude particular standpoints and prevent finer-grained understandings of the social processes of institutions.

More recently, Megan Schoen et al. examine in their chapter "Written in Homely Discourse: A Case Study of Intellectual and Institutional Identity in Teaching Genres" how the textual genres of Oakland University's writing department syllabi and assignment descriptions function to define the identities of our instructors and our institution alike. Seeking to avoid "chronicling our department's emergence in the familiar form of an administration-centric historiographic narrative" (194), the authors interrogate how our program's values and identity are enacted through the written teaching genres of individual instructors.

In doing so, the authors—all of whom are co-authors of the present chapter—began to see firsthand the value of shifting focus away from administration and toward the individuals performing work in, and on behalf of, the department. We now recognize this strategic shift in focus as part of what Smith terms "looking up" (*Institutional Ethnography as Practice* 5). As LaFrance notes, "One of the most powerful imaginative moves of IE is its insistence that we are the institution. . . . With 'standing under' (*qua* 'looking up' or 'studying up') as a foundational imaginative act, we begin to pay attention to more than simply what is happening, and we key into how what is happening takes shape as a reflection of the social" (133). LaFrance and Nicolas note that such uncovering reveals "what practices constitute the practice of the institution as we think of it, how discourse may be understood to compel and shape those practices, and how norms of practices speak to, for, and over other individuals" (131). As we see it, then, IE has the potential to vastly complicate the question "How do we do this?"—not just by confounding the agency implied by the question (who, exactly, are *we* and who are the *doers* in the stories we tell?), but also by revealing some of the micro-level particulars of *how* things are accomplished institutionally.

For this study, we sought to better understand the role of two texts that ostensibly coordinate the work of our department: *The Department of Writing and Rhetoric Faculty Handbook* (Ostergaard) and our first-year writing guide for students, *Grizz Writes: A Guide to First-Year Writing at Oakland University* (Schoen). The faculty handbook is compiled and maintained by the department chair to outline university-, college-, and department-level policies and practices for faculty. As a boss text, it functions to convey procedures and policies that coordinate the activity of contingent faculty and provides a contextual understanding of institutional practices. By contrast, *Grizz Writes* is a self-published, first-year writing textbook authored by full- and part-time faculty, edited by the WPA, and overseen by an editorial board of part-time faculty. Faculty are regularly invited to propose new chapters for the text—for which they receive a stipend—and they are regularly surveyed to find out which chapters and organizational schemes they find most effective or useful. *Grizz Writes* is constructive and communal by design, seeking to introduce faculty and students to pedagogical methods, values, and goals while attempting to account for both the diversity of faculty backgrounds and the needs of the student body.

As we demonstrate below, these two ostensible "regulatory texts" (Smith, *Institutional Ethnography: A Sociology for People* 84) may both affirm and belie the stories we have told ourselves and others about how we come to enact our disciplinary and departmental values within our institution. In the sections that follow, we briefly provide an analysis of both of these boss texts. We also discuss a survey of department faculty that provides details about how each text may be activated and resisted by individual faculty. As we find, our texts participate in surprisingly subtle and dynamic processes of activation and resistance, potentiating ruling relations in a complex "interplay among the individual, the material, and the ideological" (LaFrance 40) within our department.

ANALYZING OUR BOSS TEXTS

We first sought to describe how our institution is represented and coded into our department's primary boss texts by performing a textual analysis of them. As LaFrance reminds us,

> As texts carry ideas, language, and rhetorical frameworks
> between individuals (even those with little personal interac-
> tion) to impose notions of ideal practice and affiliation, the
> texts are not just sources of information but shapers of think-
> ing and practice. Likewise, through texts and textual practices,
> individuals are enabled to recognize, organize, and respond to
> processes of social coordination. (43)

By looking closely at the rhetorical and linguistic construction of our boss texts, we hope to reveal more about how these processes of shaping and social coordination occur.

For instance, grammatical agency—as conveyed through texts' use of the passive and active voice—offers textual traces of how actual agency is apportioned to individuals within the institution. Similarly, the use of declarative, subjunctive, and conditional moods can suggest which facets of the institution are held to be immutable and which are presumably amenable to the exercise of individual agency. The use of the imperative mood in texts can reveal who is socially authorized within the institution to issue commands, and to whom. And diectic indicators within texts can convey the relative positioning of entities in time (such as using the past, present, and future tenses), in person (such as using the first, second, and third person), in discourse (such as referring to different texts or parts of the texts themselves), but also—and most crucially for this study—within social realms (see Cruse). In the following sections, we present an examination of our boss texts to discern how our institution's various standpoints and ruling relations are coded linguistically and rhetorically within them.

THE FACULTY HANDBOOK

The handbook serves a number of administrative and rhetorical functions: (1) it is designed as a welcome to the department; (2) it is an authoritative voice overviewing policies designed to regulate instructor activity; and (3) it offers new colleagues overtly persuasive texts to promote best practices for the first-year writing program. The handbook is a heterogeneous document whose tone, syntax, and grammar shift from section to section, and even from sentence to sentence. For example, the handbook adopts a welcoming and inclusive tone in an introductory statement about department values: "Because we view written language as a form of action, worthy of careful consideration by students, teachers, and citizens, we affirm its ability to create common interests and foster the understanding of differences" (Ostergaard 6). Not unlike a United Nations declaration in its intent, this statement's use of the first-person plural pronoun, its sweeping scope, and its affirming, aspirational message seek to introduce faculty to a broader common cause that they are ostensibly united under as members of a shared discipline.

Elsewhere, first-person plural pronouns are used to further reinforce a sense of unity and common cause, even as the language switches to declarative statements and the conditional mood to convey how things ought to be done. For example:

> We expect students to understand that they are emerging
> scholars involved in academic dialogue rather than reporters
> summarizing the experts; we encourage real research writing
> for a particular purpose/audience, where students engage with
> their topics as contributors to a discussion of key issues and
> ideas. This kind of academic research is a process, and the
> course structure and instruction should emphasize process at
> least equally with product. (Ostergaard 25)

In handbook sections where the chair lays out the rationales for our program's embrace of rhetorical instruction, its dismissal of grammar instruction, and its approach to plagiarism prevention, the use of the first-person plural dominates, but it is frequently followed by use of the second person and the declarative mood as the implications for practice are drawn out in depth. In this way, the collective *we* of the department and the individual *you* of department faculty are subtly conflated, both grammatically and epistemically: "*we* all believe *this*, so as one of *us*, *you* are expected do *that*."

Beyond the introduction, a more administrative and legalistic tone pervades. For instance, passages such as the following are reprinted verbatim from the faculty bargaining agreement, complete with an attorney's instinctive concern for precise definitions and use of the legalistic verb "shall:" "A person rendering such service shall be titled 'special lecturer' and shall be represented by the union during such period. Employment periods shall be one year, commencing

August 15, renewable indefinitely. After four years of such service, employment periods shall be two years, renewable indefinitely" (Ostergaard 8). The second person is often employed when explicit directions are being given, for example, a passage about impermissible use of copyrighted material states, "You cannot reprint more than two excerpts . . . You cannot copy more than nine items . . ." (16). The word "must" appears in the handbook over 40 times, typically when the information being presented is of a particularly bureaucratic or legalistic nature: "Before beginning work at OU, all faculty must complete their employment paperwork" (15) and "Contracts must be signed and returned immediately . . . " (7).

At least a dozen times, the handbook employs the passive-voice phrase "are expected to" to frame the demands the department is making of faculty. For example,

> Special Lecturers and Lecturers in the department are
> expected to prepare syllabi, order textbooks, and construct
> their course schedules . . . Faculty are also expected to check
> and respond to OU email . . . Faculty are also expected to
> submit materials as requested for department or program
> assessment . . . Special Lecturers and Lecturers are expected to
> attend both of the department's faculty professional develop-
> ment meetings. (Ostergaard 8)

This passive voiced construction has the rhetorical and grammatical effect of obscuring who, or what, is imposing the expectations, but still providing the reader with a faint sense of their individual and professional agency. It remains unclear who is doing the expecting or just how disappointed they would be—or what institutional consequences would be in store for the faculty member—if those expectations were not met. But while the grammatical agent may remain unstated, the agency of the institution is patently clear to everyone reading those sentences, and the implication remains clear that the "expectations" being described are not actually voluntary. The reception of this text is inescapably colored by the institutional precarity of part-time faculty employment at Oakland University.

GRIZZ WRITES

Grizz Writes is intended to initiate students—and less directly, faculty—into the department's culture, values, and practices. The guide addresses a primarily student audience, typically through the use of a teacherly voice and the second person pronoun "you," as in "you will learn to join the academic conversation taking place all over our campus, and this book will serve as your first guide . . . " (Schoen 1). A bureaucratic voice is also evident in appendices that outline course policies and introduce students to campus support services. For instance, an appendix outlining the department's grade grievance policy invokes generic "students" as subjects rather than, say, individuals ("you") or members of a collective ("we"): "A student who has a complaint about a classroom situation involving an instructor teaching under the WRT rubric has, first, recourse to that instructor. Any member of the Department to whom the student makes his/her complaint must send that student directly to the instructor involved" (235). Unlike the handbook, which interleaves bureaucratic and communal authority as writers to address a reader that is both a bureaucratic subject and a member of a shared community, the student guide more strongly separates the instructive chapters from the bureaucratic edicts.

The language in the introduction to *Grizz Writes* initially addresses first-year writing students in much the same way that the handbook does. The guide asserts that:

> The writing program at OU is guided by research, theory, and best practices in the field of composition-rhetoric, and we've received national recognition for our work with first-year students. In fall 2012, our first-year writing program was awarded a Conference on College Composition and Communication Writing Program Certificate of Excellence. This award is given to only a handful of writing programs every year, and it is a testament to our exceptional faculty and innovative first year writing curriculum. (Schoen 1)

Here the guide seeks to construct—in the eyes of the student audience—the course instructor as an agent of an academic unit that is shaped by current best practices and that holds a national award for writing programs. Because faculty are included as editors of the guide on the masthead and as authors of individual chapters, their pedagogical expertise is supported by the ethos of a published textbook. *Grizz Writes* further presents a vision to students of a department culture where teachers are unified by shared pedagogical experiences, goals, and values. It depicts the pedagogical principles of the department in practice, demonstrating writing as collaborative, constructive, and reflexive.

Of course, the formal linguistic features of our department's boss texts are not accidental, nor are they simply unconsciously employed components of their respective document genres. These textual features are an important part of how they coordinate the social activity of the department, even if the ruling relations they inscribe are not always consciously perceived. But as we see in the next section in our discussion of the results of our faculty survey, the ability of boss texts to coordinate social action in our department is complicated by a number of social and material factors. We also see how "institutional ethnographers benefit from recognizing the organizational power and limitations of texts and institutional discourse, which can be rewritten, ignored, forgotten, or even lost or erased entirely" (LaFrance 40).

SURVEY RESULTS

To supplement our textual analysis of the handbook and *Grizz Writes*, we undertook a 16-question survey of our faculty to determine how these boss texts shape everyday practices. This survey was approved by Oakland University's IRB under protocol #1527158–1. Twenty-one faculty participated in the survey (six full-time and 15 part-time faculty), representing a 53% response rate. The ratio of full- to part-time respondents roughly matched the makeup of the department as whole (at the time of the survey we had 14 full-time and 32 part-time faculty). We first asked faculty to reflect on their standpoints within the institution. When recipients were asked if they felt they had the autonomy to teach their courses the way they wanted, predictable differences emerged between full- and part-time faculty: every full-time respondent (6) indicated that they had "a great deal" of autonomy, while responses from part-time faculty ranged from "very little" (1), to "somewhat" (3), to "quite a bit" (7), to "a great deal" (4). These responses suggest that both full- and part-time faculty largely feel they are trusted by department administrators to independently structure their course content and materials. While full- and part-time colleagues differed in the degree of their perceived autonomy, it is notable that none of the part-time respondents felt they had no autonomy at all. The remainder of the survey asked faculty to reflect on their interactions with the faculty handbook and *Grizz Writes*.

When asked to identify parts of the faculty handbook that were important to their teaching, only six of the 21 responding faculty members (29%) identified a specific section that they found valuable. When asked to recall when they last accessed the handbook, responses fell within three groups: eight faculty members (38%) claimed they had consulted the handbook recently, six (29%) only viewed it when they were first hired, and the remaining seven respondents (33%) admitted they had never viewed it or could not recall when they last looked at it. Of those who had consulted the handbook, the information they were seeking was about pay and contract renewals, information about syllabus language and required textbooks, and information about policies related to student issues and needs. These responses suggest our colleagues have relatively limited firsthand interactions with the handbook. While this finding is not surprising to us, it does confirm that, to the extent that the handbook acts a boss text, it does so through indirect, socially mediated channels.

While only six respondents (29%) identified a specific section of the faculty handbook that they found valuable to their teaching, 18 out of 21 instructors (86%) identified a section in *Grizz Writes* that was. Of these instructors, 15 identified two or more specific chapters, and 11 identified four or more chapters. Despite widespread reliance on *Grizz Writes* in the classroom, however, most respondents felt that it only minimally constrained their teaching—when asked to rate the degree to which the text affected what they could or could not do as an instructor, four respondents (19%) answered "somewhat," 12 (57%) answered "very little," and five (24%) answered "not at all." This suggests that while *Grizz Writes* may be our department's most central boss text—serving to coordinate the institutional activities of instruction and encoding the pedagogical values of the discipline of writing studies—it also does not deterministically impose pedagogical beliefs and practices on individuals. As one full-time faculty member responded:

> As the writing department, I think it is important to teach proper grammar rules (even if that is not the sole focus of our instruction). The "Why We Don't Teach Grammar" chapter on *Grizz Writes* needs to be updated or removed as it contains only two outdated citations (1985 [Hartwell] and 1987 [Hillocks]). If we are truly preparing students for "professional writing," then they need to know what those professional writing rules are and how they are rhetorical (just as the chapter pointed out). I feel that some students (and instructors) are using that chapter as an excuse for not educating themselves on proper grammar rules.

Here we see resistance not just to the boss text itself, but to a longstanding consensus in the academic field of composition-rhetoric. In registering their resistance to the *Grizz Writes* text and to how it is used by their colleagues, this faculty member illustrates LaFrance and Nicolas' view that "Individuals are far from powerless in the face of institutional texts" and individuals "must actively take up the discourses presented and may do so in highly unpredictable and dynamic ways" (140). This process of activation is, as LaFrance notes, "as unpredictable and dynamic as the people we study" (44).

We also see in the above response—from a full-time colleague—a reminder that individual activation is required not only for this particular text to participate in the enactment of ruling relations within our institution, but for texts to be activated within the broader discipline as well ("outdated citations" or not). As Ruth Book characterizes it in Chapter 3 of this collection, resistance "is not merely stubbornness or inflexibility, but rather comes about from disjunctures in the roles that instructors play in the institution and the values that accompany those roles." Moreover, as LaFrance notes, "an individual's social alliances, experiences, and sensibilities play an important role in how that individual negotiates everyday institutional settings (such as classrooms, programs, or departments). Our local practices may or may not reflect the ruling realities prescribed by disciplinary or professional discourses" (118).

IN THE SPACES BETWEEN: FINDING THE BOSS OF US

Both the handbook and *Grizz Writes* inscribe a complex set of ruling relations in our institution. The handbook operates both in its substance (its recitation of legal/bureaucratic polices as imposed from above and "best practices" for instruction as advanced by a broader community of writing studies scholars) and in its style (its diectic indicators, the very grammar of the text) to reciprocally co-instantiate the positionings and activities of instructor, administrator, student, etc. As we see in this study, however, the handbook text is not often experienced firsthand by our faculty: few faculty agreed that the handbook constrains their instruction and even fewer conceded to having read the text at all. As Smith notes, though, texts that remain unseen or are "otherwise out of action, exist *in potentia* but their potentiating is in time and in action, whether in ongoing text-reader conversations or in how the 'having read' enters into the organization of what is to come." ("Texts" 174). We believe that the handbook largely functions in this way within our department, achieving a seemingly paradoxical "action-at-a-distance" through social processes among department faculty rather than through unmediated exposure to the text itself. These social processes occur "among people who are situated in particular places at particular times, and not as 'meaning' or 'norms'" (Smith, "Texts" 161).

Meanwhile, the communally authored textbook *Grizz Writes* enjoys much more direct engagement with faculty, both pedagogically as a classroom tool and as a collective editorial endeavor. Like the handbook, this text serves to advance ruling relations for instructor, administrator, student, etc. But *Grizz Writes* differs from the handbook in at least two important ways with regard to faculty agency: even as it is a required textbook, it provides a sense of textual ownership by dint of being communally authored and edited and its modular design permits faculty to exercise some degree of professional agency as instructors by simply not assigning chapters that they do not want to. A diverse faculty committee is charged with soliciting and selecting *Grizz Writes* chapters, which are all authored by our faculty, and faculty receive a stipend for their writing. Additionally, some portion of the faculty exercise their agency through pedagogical choice: when asked if there were any chapters of *Grizz Writes* that they deliberately avoided for any reason, two-thirds of respondents (67%, *n* = 18) said no, but 27% expressly named chapters that they avoid assigning. (In a parallel question, all respondents expressly named chapters that are particularly valuable to their teaching.) So *Grizz Writes* potentiates ruling relations that allow agentive space for our faculty to act out of concert with one another or with institutional prerogatives—even as the scope of action permitted within that space remains circumscribed by other operative ruling relations (including the fact that *Grizz Writes* is required of all first-year writing courses in the first place).

Looking beyond these two boss texts, the survey reveals some of the other significant ruling relations in our department. Respondents were asked to numerically rank the following items according to which they rely on most for information about teaching in the department: the handbook, *Grizz Writes*, the writing program administrator, the department chair, colleagues, and eSpace, the department's online repository of teaching resources. The top-rated source was colleagues (with an average numerical ranking of 2.53, with 1 indicating the highest rank). The writing program administrator was second-highest (3.00), followed very closely by the department chair (3.15) and eSpace (3.24). Notably, *Grizz Writes* (3.62) and the handbook (5.00) were the two lowest-ranked sources of information. In response to open-ended questions about the influence of our boss texts, one respondent noted "Most of what I feel I can or cannot do as an instructor is picked up through conversations with my colleagues. I very rarely consult the handbook for that information." Another respondent noted, "I consulted with my colleagues more on department policy and practices than [what] instructors can and cannot do."

These findings are consistent with interviews conducted by Schoen et al. in their chapter "Written in Homely Discourse." In that study, the authors report that 11 out of 13 of Oakland University writing department instructors (85%) cited the role of their colleagues in shaping their course instruction, acknowledging that even informal conversations with colleagues significantly impacted their syllabi, assignment descriptions, and pedagogy. A major takeaway of that study was that the material context of writing instruction, including physical infrastructure such as office space, is essential for the "discourse community's ability to communicate and collaboratively innovate pedagogical genres." As is the case at most universities, space is among the scarcest campus resources at our institution. Unfortunately, our department has been forced to physically separate our full- and part-time faculty into separate, inequitable campus locations. A portion of our part-time faculty (over-)occupy a small number of basement offices where full-time faculty occupy individual offices on the third floor, while other part-time faculty are relegated to a separate building across campus. The

ruling relations inscribed by these divisions within space are not of our making, and the odious upstairs/downstairs/cross-campus social dynamic it fosters
is despised among our department faculty.[1] But this ruling relation is writ large
within the text of our campus itself, serving very powerfully—and materially—
to coordinate department activity on administration's terms and to determine
the possibilities for social and intellectual interchange.

This is an important reminder that our department's boss texts act, react,
and interact with one another in complex ways. To be sure, none of us suffered
the delusion that our faculty were reading the handbook from cover to cover,
internalizing its dictums, and instantly absorbing its schematic textual represen-
tations of the organization and conforming to the institutional identity depicted
therein. And no one believed that our instructors were obediently following
Grizz Writes as their one and only sourcebook for pedagogical knowledge. Still,
all of our prior scholarship about Oakland's writing department—our accounts
of program building, curricular design, program administration, instructional
space design, and so on—tacitly presumed a top-down imposition of disciplinary values, processes, and best practices from a larger scholarly community
onto a local institution of our design. We did not attend to *how things happen*
(LaFrance 40)—our accounts did not capture the nuanced ways ruling relations
are enacted at our institution and certainly none of them acknowledged the
ways faculty might resist, riff on, short circuit, or circumvent the ruling relations
imposed on them. As LaFrance observes,

> The actualities of pedagogical practice, I disclose, while often
> initially driven by national conversations of best practice and
> scholarly concern, take actual shape in relation to a number of
> shifting material conditions and systems of value—a recogni-
> tion often missing in our field's conversations about effective
> writing pedagogy. (135)

From the literal texts of our handbook and *Grizz Writes* to the material text
of our office buildings, IE helps us to see our program as a more nuanced complex of ruling relations than our prior scholarship admitted.

As we write this, our department is in the process of approving a new diversity, equity, inclusion, and anti-oppression policy (Carmichael et al.). This DEIA

---

1   Michele LaFrance and Anicca Cox explore the role of campus architecture to inscribe
systems of labor and social inequality in "Brutal(ist) Meditations: Space and Labor-Movement
in a Writing Program." They describe a situation nearly identical to ours that occurred in their
department at UMass Dartmouth: an upstairs/downstairs hierarchical division between full-time
and contingent faculty. As they describe, on their campus "professional marginalization is built
quite literally into the concrete" (282).

policy is an institutional product, having been authored by an *ad hoc* committee after many months of collaborative research, deliberation, and review. The policy was submitted to our department's governing committee for formal ratification and is now slated to achieve the same institutional and bureaucratic status as, say, our policies on who or who not may use the department photocopier. The DEIA policy obviously transcends and vastly outweighs the photocopier use policy, and it portends much greater liberatory and transformative potential for the institution. But, as an institutional product, the DEIA policy will undergo the same textual fate as all of the other policies in our department: it will be printed on the same pages in the same typeface as the other official policies enshrined in our department's boss texts.

But to understand how those policies will differ in their uptake—that is, how they are activated or not by individual agents of the institution and how social processes shape such activation—is to understand how these policies' textual fate differs from their institutional fate. The methods of IE, we believe, allow us to appreciate the nuanced and nondeterministic ways that policy texts move from the pages of our workaday department documents to coordinate the material and ideological activities of individuals within our institution. Of course, we believe that we have a moral calling to develop the kind of institutional self-understanding that only IE can foster. We also believe that IE can help us to strategically position initiatives like our DEIA policy, ensuring that an essential statement of our department's values does not languish on the pages of our boss texts but is instead enacted by individuals throughout our curricula, pedagogy, administration, and department relationships. Institutional efforts like our DEIA policy are often criticized—rightfully—for making performative, hortatory declarations that ultimately do little to inspire perceptible, material changes to the *status quo*. But with a fuller understanding how ruling relations are potentiated and come to coordinate our activity, we come to recognize that the official adoption of a policy marks a midpoint in a complex social process of uptake and activation, not its end. In this way, IE may help us to ensure that our DEIA policy will have an actual lasting affect within and upon our institution.

WORKS CITED

Allan, Elizabeth, et al. "The Source of Our Ethos: Using Evidence-Based Practices to Affect a Program-Wide Shift from 'I Think' to 'We Know.'" *Composition Forum*, vol.32, no. 32, 2015. https://compositionforum.com/issue/32/oakland.php.

Andersen, Wallis. "Outside the English Department: Oakland University's Writing Program and the Writing and Rhetoric Major." *What We Are Becoming:*

Developments in Undergraduate Writing Majors, edited by Greg A. Giberson and Thomas A. Moriarty, Utah State UP, 2015, pp. 67–80.

Carmichael, Felicita, et al. "Commitment to Diversity, Equity, Inclusion, and Anti-Oppression." *Oakland University Department of Writing and Rhetoric*, 2021. Policy document.

Chong, Felicia, and Jim Nugent. "A New Major in the Shadow of the Past: The Professional Writing Track at Oakland University." *Programmatic Perspectives*, vol. 7, no. 2, 2015, pp. 173–88.

Cruse, Alan. *Meaning in Language: An Introduction to Semantics and Pragmatics*. 3rd ed., Oxford UP, 2011.

Driscoll, Dana Lynn, and Marshall Kitchens. "Engaging in Communities of Practice: Supplementing Community-Based Service Learning with Online Reflection in a Peer Tutoring Course." *Community Engagement 2.0?: Dialogues on the Future of the Civic in the Disrupted University*, edited by Scott L. Crabill and Dan Butin, Palgrave Macmillan, 2014, pp. 41–55.

Giberson, Greg A., et al., editors. *Writing Majors: Eighteen Program Profiles*. Utah State UP, 2015.

Giberson, Greg A., et al. "A Changing Profession Changing a Discipline: Junior Faculty and the Undergraduate Major." *Composition Forum*, no. 20, 2009.

Griffith, Alison I., and Dorothy E. Smith. *Under New Public Management: Institutional Ethnographies of Changing Front-Line Work*, U of Toronto P, 2014.

Hartwell, Patrick. "Grammar, Grammars, and the Teaching of Grammar." *College English*, vol. 47, no. 2, 1985, pp. 105–27.

Hillocks, George. "Synthesis of Research on Teaching Writing." *Educational Leadership*, vol. 44, pp. 71–82, 1987.

Kraemer, Beth, et al. "Partnership as Process: Moving Toward an Integrated Undergraduate Writing Curriculum Using the Association of College & Research Libraries Framework for Information Literacy for Higher Education." *Rewired: Research-Writing Partnerships within the Frameworks*, edited by Randall McClure, Association of College and Research Libraries Publications, 2016, pp. 153–74.

LaFrance, Michelle. *Institutional Ethnography: A Theory of Practice for Writing Studies Researchers*. Utah State UP, 2019.

LaFrance, Michelle, and Anicca Cox. "Brutal(ist) Meditations: Space and Labor-Movement in a Writing Program." *Contingency, Exploitation, and Solidarity: Labor and Action in English Composition*, edited by Seth Kahn, et al., The WAC Clearinghouse / UP of Colorado, 2017, pp. 279–301. https://doi.org/10.37514/per-b.2017.0858.2.18.

LaFrance, Michelle, and Melissa Nicolas. "Institutional Ethnography as Materialist Framework for Writing Program Research and the Faculty-Staff Work Standpoints Project." *College Composition and Communication*, vol. 64, no. 1, 2012, pp. 130–50.

Nugent, Jim. "Introduction." *Writing Majors: Eighteen Program Profiles*, edited by Greg A., Jim Nugent et al., Utah State UP, 2015, pp. 1–9.

Ostergaard, Lori, editor. *The Department of Writing and Rhetoric Faculty Handbook*. Oakland University Department of Writing and Rhetoric, 2019.

Ostergaard, Lori, and Elizabeth Allan. "From Falling Through the Cracks to Pulling Through: Moving from a Traditional Remediation Model Toward a Multi-Layered Support Model for Basic Writing." *Journal of Basic Writing*, vol. 35, no. 1, 2017, pp. 44–83.

Ostergaard, Lori, et al. "Using the Framework to Shape Basic Writing Students' College Readiness." *The Framework for Success in Postsecondary Writing: Scholarship and Applications*, edited by Sherry Rankins-Robertson, et al., Parlor P, 2017, pp. 257–82.

Ostergaard, Lori A., and Greg A. Giberson. "Unifying Program Goals: Developing and Implementing a Writing and Rhetoric Major at Oakland University." *Composition Forum*, vol. 22, 2010.

Ostergaard, Lori, et al. "Oakland University's Major in Writing and Rhetoric." *Writing Majors: Eighteen Program Profiles*, edited by Greg Giberson, et al., Utah State UP, 2015, pp. 73–84.

Schoen, Megan, editor. Grizz Writes: *A Guide to First-Year Writing at Oakland University*. 8th ed., Fountainhead Press, 2019.

Schoen, Megan, et al. "Written in Homely Discourse: A Case Study of Intellectual and Institutional Identity in Teaching Genres." *Writing the Classroom: Pedagogical Documents as Rhetorical Genres*, edited by Stephen Neaderhiser, Utah State UP, 2022, pp. 193–211. https://doi.org/10.7330/9781646422920.c010.

Schoen, Megan, and Lori Ostergaard. "From 'Expendable' to Credentialed: Empowering Contingent Faculty through the HLC's Guidelines for Faculty Qualifications." *Transformations: Change Work Across Writing Programs, Pedagogies, and Practices*, edited by Holly Hassel and Kirsti Cole, Utah State UP, 2021, pp. 53–71.

Smith, Dorothy E. *Institutional Ethnography: A Sociology for People*. AltaMira, 2005.

———. *Institutional Ethnography as Practice*. Rowman and Littlefield, 2006.

———. "Texts and the Ontology of Organizations and Institutions." *Studies in Cultures, Organizations, and Societies*, vol. 7, no. 2, 2001, pp. 159–98.

Walwema, Josephine, and Dana Lynn Driscoll. "Activating the Uptake of Prior Knowledge Through Metacognitive Awareness: An Exploratory Study of Writing Transfer in Documentation and Source Use in Professional Writing Courses." *Programmatic Perspectives*, vol. 7, no. 1, 2015, pp. 21–42.

CHAPTER 4.

"THE TENSION'S IN THIS ROOM!:" NEGOTIATION AND RESISTANCE IN IE FOCUS GROUPS

Ruth Book

Rochester Institute of Technology

Institutional ethnography has much to offer writing program administrators generally, but perhaps one of the most important things it provides is an approach to difference and resistance as an asset. IE presupposes that there will be "disjunctions, divergences, and distinctions" in any site and provides an opening for researchers to study the complex negotiations that members of the institution undertake as part of their everyday work (LaFrance 35). Writing program administrators are typically no strangers to resistance, sometimes coming from multiple directions at once: students, teachers, administrators, or other stakeholders. While new TAs' resistance to first-year writing program pedagogies has been well documented by WPA scholars, resistance does not simply dissipate once the TAs are no longer "new teachers." Though these feelings may shift and change as teachers' own experiences do, instructor resistance and ambivalence often remain—especially when a writing program undergoes a significant change in its curriculum and identity, which was the exigence for developing the study that I describe in this chapter.

My purpose here is to show how institutional ethnography allows researchers to uncover and examine the usually invisible negotiations that occur on the interindividual level between individuals and the institution. In the course of their everyday work, individuals constantly negotiate their responsibilities, experiences, and identities not only within the institution but also collaboratively among each other. Throughout this chapter, I show how institutional ethnography provides a way for WPAs to view how instructor resistance is performed and negotiated within the writing program, and I suggest that focus groups are a method of data collection particularly well suited to IE inquiry because they show these resistances and negotiations *as they happen*. While the institution presents instructors with particular roles and guides their practice in those roles through institutional circuitry, instructors' identities and identifications with the writing program are multiple and shifting. IE provides a method for WPAs to

DOI: https://doi.org/10.37514/PER-B.2023.2029.2.04

honor the lived experiences of the members of the writing program, including a diversity of (dis)identifications with and resistances to the writing program.

I begin with a research narrative of my study that provides context about the local writing program and its members. I then briefly explain the potential for focus groups as a method for exploring resistance and negotiation in the writing program before turning to a discussion of particular moments of instructor resistance that are mediated by local and extralocal concerns based on their standpoints in the institution. Throughout this chapter, my goal is to consider how institutional ethnography can help WPAs open lines of inquiry into the ways instructors negotiate the various roles they fulfill within the institution, form their individual and collective identities as teachers, and experience ambivalence and resistance to programmatic values and practices.

RESEARCH CONTEXT AND NARRATIVE

The first-year writing program where I conducted this study had approximately 85 instructors at the main campus; of the 105 course sections taught in the Fall 2017 semester, when data collection began, slightly more than half were taught by graduate students (both M.A. and Ph.D.) in literary studies, medieval studies, and rhetoric and composition, with another 40% taught by adjunct faculty, and only 3% taught by full-time faculty. In addition to the main campus, there are also four regional campuses, each with a faculty writing coordinator and a robust early college experience program, where FYW is delivered in more than a hundred high schools across the state. Having been both an instructor[1] and graduate student administrator in this program, I was uniquely positioned to investigate the identity of the program as both a participant and a creator of the collective identity of this writing program as it underwent a significant shift.

Beginning with the arrival of a new director in the 2016–2017 academic year, the writing program began transitioning to a multimodal curriculum. The program's website describes the initiative as "a component of the FYW program designed to teach rhetorical composition practices with a diverse range of technologies and communicative modes" ("Writing Across Technology"). When I began this study in Fall 2017, the transition was already in motion, and by the following year, new graduate instructors were fully trained by the summer workshop staff in multimodal composition in their week-long orientation and fall-semester pedagogy course and practicum. Returning instructors had also

---

1   I use the word "instructor" to refer to anyone who teaches FYW at our institution, which is common practice in our program. Though graduate students teaching in our program are classified as "graduate teaching assistants" (GTAs) by the university, they design and implement all of their teaching.

begun to implement digital and multimodal elements into their courses with varying degrees of engagement since the new director's arrival.

I collected data across four semesters (Fall 2017–Spring 2019), including ten years of training materials, (beginning with the year that the first participant entered the program), focus groups with instructors, and interviews with the writing program's directors, graduate assistant directors, and regional campus coordinators. I used the training materials (called "resource books") to develop an initial coding scheme for analyzing the materials and the responses from instructors in the focus groups, according to their stated values and practices as teachers. I invited all active instructors via email and paper flyers. Twenty-eight instructors responded and participated in six randomly populated focus groups that explored the ways instructors felt that they embodied the values, goals, and practices of the still-shifting program. In our focus groups, I asked instructors to reflect on their experiences to discuss what roles they fulfilled in their teaching and whom they identified with or were influenced by as they continued to craft their own teaching identities.

Choosing to use focus groups rather than individual interviews with instructors was not simply an efficiency measure; they proved essential to the project since my goal was to investigate the relationships that instructors sustain and the ways that they negotiate their experiences in their current institutional situation. For reasons that will be explained in the later sections, the focus groups were the site of most of the significant insights for this project, despite or because of their messiness. In addition to the focus groups, interviews with the WPAs and the programmatic documents were useful in establishing the ruling relations of the site and seeing the trajectory of the identity of the writing program across time.

Many studies of the developing identities of writing teachers begin with new graduate instructors, many of whom are teaching for the first time, as they navigate the difficulty of being teachers and students through their first semester or year (see, for example, Ebest; Grouling; Restaino). My study, by contrast, looks at the ways in which all instructors' identities shape and are shaped by a change in the program's identity resulting from a new director and a change in curriculum. As I've found through this research, writing instructors often take up certain aspects of the collective identity of the program to which they belong while upholding their own values and goals —sometimes in addition or in opposition to those of the writing program, all of which contribute to the performance of their identity as teachers of writing. As they manage the expectations set out for them by the institution, many instructors find creative and subversive ways to fulfill their roles as teachers of writing. While much of what happens in the day-to-day experience of writing instructors is invisible to WPAs, I suggest in the next section that focus groups provide a social and rhetorical site for exploring the negotiations that shape the professional and local identities of writing instructors.

FOCUS GROUPS AND IE

Together with other forms of data collection, focus groups can provide the institutional ethnographer a view into the institutional negotiations that writing program members participate in *as they are happening*. Focus groups might be a method of data collection especially suited to institutional ethnography because of the interactional nature of the meeting itself. Focus groups aren't merely "group interviews," and, as Sue Wilkinson has noted, researchers should be prepared to analyze the results of focus groups not only in terms of *what* is said (content) but also *how* it is said (interaction). A focus group is not a clear window into the goings on of the institution; instead, a focus group meeting is itself an enactment of the negotiations the individuals experience within the institution.

For the institutional ethnographer, focus groups have much to tell us about the strategic, rhetorical interactions among the participants, including how they are positioning themselves within the conversation, how they interact with others, and how they co-construct meaning within the institutional site. Focus groups, when "sensitively analyzed," can "offer insights into the relational aspects of self, the processes by which meanings and knowledge are constructed through interaction with others, and the ways in which social inequalities are produced and perpetuated through talk" (Wilkinson 123). Wilkinson reminds us that focus group data are just as constructed as surveys or interviews are, with the added element of interaction. A focus group is an event occurring within the institution, not somehow outside of it, and therefore it is a site where the program's identity is negotiated and shaped in real time among the participants and moderator. My own presence as a moderator and member of the community surely shaped the participants' experience, though not in a quantifiable way; it is likely that preexisting relationships with me and each other led to both a willingness to disclose their experiences as well as some instances of careful negotiation and politeness in crafting their responses sensitively. In any case, my asking them to participate in this research study shaped the way they perceived the writing program and their place within it. Indeed, the research site is never undisturbed by a focus group taking place. Instructors' performances in the focus groups were instances that shaped the program's identity for me and for the other instructors who were present. As I analyzed the data from the focus groups, I attended to the ways that the participants constructed responses to the questions that displayed both their particular identities and practices as well as how they interacted and collaborated with me and each other in the space.

NEGOTIATING PROGRAMMATIC
VALUES AND PRACTICES

In order to determine the key values and practices of the local writing program, I gathered ten years of resource books, training manuals that a team of experienced graduate student teachers revise each summer in preparation for new-instructor orientation. As a product of sustained collaboration, these resource books often contain the program's most current values and practices, and they were especially useful in understanding how the program communicated its curricular changes to teachers. Ranging from around 400 pages (in 2011) to a more concise 75 pages (in 2018), the resource books contained descriptions of the course outcomes, guiding principles, sample assignments and lesson plans, and suggestions for approaching teaching and assessing writing.

At the program level, the resource books constitute what Alice Griffith and Dorothy Smith refer to as a "boss text," a higher-order text that shapes and mediates the work of individuals within the institution. While there are certainly other boss texts that shape instructors' work at the program, university, and disciplinary level, the resource books are significant in that they have "accrue[d] a particular type of authority within local settings, as they circulate ideals of accountability, professionalism, and disciplinarity" (LaFrance 80). These documents bear much of the burden of introducing instructors to the identity of the writing program and certainly shape their everyday work, even if indirectly. Not every instructor reads the resource books cover-to-cover or in the same manner, but their significance rests in that they are a shared resource taken up by individuals as they go about their work; they inform the individual and collaborative practice of teaching writing in the local writing program.

A writing program is made up of, at least in part, the documents and textual artifacts that circulate among its various stakeholders. Christopher Burnham and Susanne Green suggest that a writing program's identity is "embedded, if not clearly represented, in program literature, from catalog materials and common course syllabi to department and program (and faculty and GA) websites" (176). But these texts, themselves, do not constitute the identity of the program in its entirety. The replicability of texts is central to the ontology of organizations and institutions, according to Smith ("Texts"), because they "provide for the standardized recognizability of people's doings *as* organizational or institutional" (160; emphasis added). The institution comes into being, as Dylan Dryer explains, as it is "materially (re)constituted in the everyday uptakes of recurrent textual forms" (653). The texts themselves must be activated by members of the institution as they go about their work (Smith *Institutional*).

To approach analyzing these programmatic materials, I developed a qualitative coding scheme that cataloged all of the values and practices discussed in the resource books. Though it is outside the scope of this chapter to explore in great detail, there were clear ways that the resource books connected with extralocal ruling relations that establish how and why we teach writing in particular ways. For example, disciplinary texts such as the "Framework for Success in Postsecondary Writing," NCTE position statements, and the ACRL's "Framework for Information Literacy for Higher Education," all informed particular values and practices, such as developing habits of mind, encouraging multimodal composition, and outlining practices for ethical research. This catalog of values and practices allowed me to map significant programmatic changes across time and served as a backdrop to explore the instructors' conversations in the six focus groups.

After I had developed a system for cataloging the values and practices recommended in the resource books, I turned to the focus group transcripts to see the ways that the values and practices outlined in these training materials shaped instructors' understanding of their work as writing teachers. In the first round of coding, I analyzed the focus group conversations by coding their transcripts according to the values and practices established in the official documents. Across the six focus groups, participants discussed key values and practices that appeared in the official discourse of the program: *Reading, collaboration, rhetorical awareness, multimodal composition, assessment, writing* (as an activity in class), *multimodality, revision, reflection & metacognition,* and *process writing* all emerged strongly as key terms across both the resource books and the focus groups. Tracing the key terms, values, and practices of the program through the resource books and focus groups allowed me to see how instructors were engaging with and embodying official program discourses in the construction of their individual and collective identities as instructors. LaFrance suggests that "tracing key terms is one pathway to understanding how the specific faces of an institution are co-created in the space between larger social discourses and individual standpoints" (113). By tracing these key terms as they emerged in the focus groups, I was able to identify what the writing instructors valued based on how they responded to questions and interacted with each other through their identity performances and negotiations in the focus groups.

I began the six focus groups by asking instructors to write about and then share their primary goals as writing instructors. Then, I asked them to continue by talking about what they viewed as the goals and values of the program in general. By the third focus group, I opened this second question with a joke that it wasn't a test, trying to ease some of the tension of performing for each other and for me, but their nervous laughter indicated to me that they were, in fact, worried it was a test to be evaluated by me and their peers around the table.

Though I'd assured them that their responses would be private and deidentified to everyone outside of the room, my own role as the graduate student writing program administrator (and in many cases, my differently positioned role as peer or friend) was certainly not lost on participants. As I was analyzing these moments, the complex rhetorical nature of the focus groups became clear: They were inhabiting this space with me, an administrator, and their peer instructors, which invariably shaped the ways that they performed their identities as instructors. The focus groups themselves were still operating within the institution, rather than as a neutral site to gather data. Throughout the focus groups, participants negotiated their participation in ways that showed they were engaged members of the writing program by aligning with the espoused values and practices of the writing program, as well as instructors capable of agency and independence by subverting or flouting those values and practices.

As they answered this question about the program's values and practices, each instructor answered with something that was recognizably part of the identity of the writing program but that was also something that marked their own teaching identity as unique. Their responses to this question showed that each instructor was performing an act of identification with the writing program while asserting and maintaining their own individuality. I asked the question to twenty-eight instructors, and I received twenty-eight different responses to what they believed were the most important values and practices of the writing program. Some emphasized writing process, reading and critical literacy, multimodal composition, academic writing, information literacy, and metacognitive practices in writing, among other values and practices. Though the list of values and practices from the resource book was extensive, nearly all of them were discussed at some point during the six focus groups with instructors. The wide range of responses suggests that instructors were not merely reciting what they felt they ought to value, but rather choosing to emphasize elements of the shared community that resonated with their own histories, backgrounds, and goals as writing instructors.

After I accounted for the ways instructors discussed the "official" values and practices, I marked places in the transcripts where the coding scheme did not account for the content of the focus group conversations. Once I had refined these moments into categories, 11 new values and practices emerged, which are shown in Table 4.1. While some values or practices were more idiosyncratic (e.g., self-expression, appearing only once), others represented a significant amount of the conversation between instructors in focus groups. For example, there were 49 coded references to *affective or emotion work* as integral to their pedagogical practices and values, spanning topics such as instilling confidence in student writers, managing student stress, responding to students with enthusiasm and generosity, and other forms of emotional labor. Deeply connected to this kind of emotion work was a discussion of *embodiment*, including the ways that differences in gender, sexuality, ability, and race informed their teaching and how physical and material space and resources shaped their interactions with students. These additional values and practices revealed the embodied work experiences of instructors in the writing program and ways that they negotiated their own lived experiences within and outside of the traditional classroom.

Table 4.1. New Value and Practice Codes from Focus Groups

New Value and Practice Codes from Focus Groups	Number of Coding References
Self-expression	1
Critical literacy	3
Invention	4
Fairness and equity	6
Critical thinking	8
Page requirement	9
Political engagement	10
Play & experimentation	19
Embodiment	20
Teaching for transfer	23
Affective & emotion work	49

Isolating the new values and practices provided a way of understanding the limits of official discourses (e.g., training manuals) for describing the lived, embodied experiences of instructors. As I will explore in the next section, these additional values and practices also uncovered some tensions instructors had with these official discourses, especially when their deeply held values, stemming from their embodied experiences or disciplinary backgrounds, came into conflict with the program's espoused values.[2] It is not surprising that a training and resource manual does not encapsulate the affective and embodied work of teaching writing and belonging to a writing program, but we can see from the focus group conversations how significant these additional values and practices were for instructors as they navigated their day-to-day experience. In concert with other codes, (e.g., *political engagement*) *affective & emotion work* and

---

2   For a discussion of how instructors negotiate tensions between boss texts and their embodied experiences of their work, see Elisabeth Miller's chapter in this collection. Miller shows how one particularly powerful boss text and ruling relation loomed large for workers in a community writing center even as they felt it inadequately addressed the very real and embodied needs of the community with whom they worked.

embodiment revealed the complexities of instructors' identifications with the program's values and practices.

EMBODIMENT, DISCIPLINARITY, AND RESISTANCE

Embodiment and the affective aspects of teaching emerged as an important consideration for writing instructors in the focus group discussions, with 69 unique references across all six meetings combined. Though embodiment and emotions were not connected explicitly to values or practices mentioned in the official program materials, these considerations emerged as significant to how instructors viewed their work. For example, some instructors shared how their different embodiments and experiences shaped the teaching work that they do and what they value in the classroom. Among other topics, instructors expressed that gender, race, sexuality, and disability shaped their experience in the classroom and writing program. One instructor, James, described his overall goals in teaching writing as connected to the goals of the program:

> I think I'm interested in that space, making quote unquote
> "inquiry," but I put like—*I borrowed the terms from First-Year
> Writing*, right—like, critical literacy, rhetorical awareness, that
> I think are like very important. And essentially, right, like,
> hopefully being able to develop sustained, concrete arguments
> that make use of texts in ethical and responsible ways.

In describing the terms he "borrowed from First-Year Writing," this instructor shows his connection to the program while maintaining some agency in how he chooses to interact with the values of the program. While he expresses here that he emphasizes inquiry, critical literacy, and rhetorical awareness, these values are mediated by and negotiated alongside other emphases on affect, experimentation, play, and embodiment throughout the rest of the focus group. Later, he shares that for him, "Affect becomes a very sort of critical tool. And emotions—how do you feel?—that becomes a sort of way into the conversation, so making use of that. I also think to denaturalize some of the, like, straight modes of writing." For James, the experience of working as a queer scholar also shapes his priorities in the writing classroom. Maintaining these two sets of goals, ones informed by the writing program and others by his scholarly interests and approach, did not seem to create feelings of tension or resistance for James (or, at least, he did not express that they did in our meeting). There were other moments, though, where instructors' roles or embodied experiences did conflict with what they viewed as the values of the program.

In some cases, the affective and embodied elements of their work raised ambivalence or resistance from instructors. Many instructors emphasized emotional labor as something that they felt was part of their work of teaching writing, even if they sometimes felt ambivalent about that work. Emotional and affective labor is not officially or institutionally part of the work of teaching writing—it does not appear in job descriptions, training materials, or messages from the program leadership. Still, this work emerged as significant for instructors across the focus groups. Multiple instructors, for instance, mentioned that alleviating student anxiety was a key component of how they see their work, and, as a product of that, they expressed a goal of increasing students' confidence in their identity as writers.

For some instructors, the ways they went about alleviating students' anxiety sometimes, they felt, ran counter to some of the expressed goals of the first-year Writing program. When I asked one focus group about what goals, values or objectives they had in addition or in contrast to the FYW goals they had already named, they continued to discuss this affective goal from earlier in the conversation:

> **Riley:** We talked a lot about student anxiety, and that's something that I don't think first-year writing necessarily directly addresses.
>
> **Kate:** And I think a lot of the way that instructors address student anxiety is through talking to them about formal strategies, and I think that that's something that's not probably— it's, like, consciously not prioritized by the first-year writing program.
>
> **Riley:** Yeah, that's actively sort of suppressed.
>
> **Kate:** Yeah, so, that suggests to me a kind of disjunction of goals or priorities.
>
> **Riley:** I understand why first-year writing does it, right, because they don't want us to be teaching the way that [their previous institutions] or whatever does, where it's this very structured, like, "this is an introduction, these are the ways that introductions work, please write your sentences following this model." Like, I understand that they don't want that autopilot sort of course, but there is definitely a place for strategies or for talking to students—like, even getting them to understand that you can use the structure of a paper to get the point across in the same way you use the prose.

In this conversation, Riley and Kate collaboratively work through the "disjunction" between their own, which they appeared to share in common, and the writing program's goals or priorities. The program's materials and messages from the director discouraged instructors from focusing on rules of grammar, formatting, or essay structure in favor of encouraging inquiry-based writing projects. In the conversation above, "formal strategies" is a euphemism that the other instructors understand to stand in for templates or conventional essay structures. Cognizant of the context of the focus group conversation, they quickly acknowledge their understanding and identification with the writing program while expressing their resistance to or tension against the program's typical practice. They also both bring their previous experience in other writing programs to the fore in this conversation and emphatically distance themselves from their previous experiences, perhaps as a way of creating a shared identification with the others in the focus group conversation.

In this conversation, the participants worked collaboratively in the focus group exchange to explain their resistance to a program practice (not emphasizing "formal strategies") and the ways that it connected to an overarching goal of providing support to students and alleviating anxiety. In Chapter 3 of this volume, Nugent et al. explain the significance of peer relationships as instructors acculturate to a writing program or department and learn to navigate the social rules of the space. Drawing on responses to an open-ended faculty survey question, they reveal how policy is often mediated through conversations with colleagues rather than through direct consultation with a boss text, such as a handbook. These instructors' interaction in this conversation also shows the ways that focus groups can be useful in understanding how members of the writing program are engaging with each other and with their conceptualization of the institution. Even when she was explaining a tension or "disjunction," as Kate put it, with the practices of the writing program, Riley maintained that she understood why "first-year writing does it" in that way. As Jocelyn Hollander explains, "focus groups can tell us what people say in particular social contexts and how group meaning, consensus, or dissensus is constructed" but "they do not reliably tell us what individuals think or feel. Therefore, no group composition can ensure 'honest' disclosure" (628). Institutional ethnographers might be more comfortable with this statement than many other researchers because our goal is not to strive toward "truth" in an objective sense but to gather data toward coming to understand the ways people's lives and work are organized at the local and extralocal levels. Because they understand that the institution itself is textually mediated and constantly shifting based on standpoint, IE researchers are well positioned to approach focus groups (and, indeed, all of their data) as rhetorical and socially constructed. In this case, we can see

that instructors' resistances or ambivalences are motivated by other goals—
here, alleviating student anxiety—and they carefully construct their responses
to frame their experience as understanding of the program's values and practices
even when they disagree.

The transition to a more multimodal curriculum created ambivalence and
resistance from instructors on both technical and ideological grounds. While
some instructors worried about how to assign, create, or assess multimodal writing, others wondered about the underlying purposes behind the shift. *Political
engagement* and *teaching for transfer* were two values that many teachers discussed as significant for motivating their teaching experiences, though these are
not explicitly discussed in the resource books or other programmatic materials.
In one focus group conversation, two participants, Samantha and Cassandra,
discussed the tension between "political" and "practical" (or "professional")
approaches to teaching writing:

> **Cassandra:** So, I think that the word "practical" is a point
> of tension in this program right now. And maybe this comes
> from, I was in pedagogy [the practicum/training course] with
> [a previous director], right? But I also study the corporate
> university, so that word freaks me out.
>
> **Ruth:** And so how are you, how is that word circulating for
> you? Where is that coming from?
>
> **Cassandra:** Well, let's connect it to maybe, like, the multi-
> modal changes that are happening, which are often phrased
> as being more practical genres of writing than the traditional
> essay.
>
> **Samantha:** I will say I agree that's definitely a tension that
> I've seen, but it's also, I don't know if it's like, different years,
> necessarily, who came in with what teacher [of the practicum/
> training course], because I know several people who were in
> [the course] with me who have the same aversion to practical-
> ity. I'm deeply, deeply in love with practicality.
>
> **Cassandra:** The tension's in this room!
>
> **Samantha:** I know!

Though this was a light, joking conversation in one of the focus groups, it
revealed instructors' perceptions of tensions among multiple values and motivations central to their teaching. Cassandra's response to the program's change to a
more multimodal curriculum was informed by her disciplinary research on the
corporate university and her concerns about transitioning to a more "practical"

and instrumental approach to teaching writing. Throughout the focus group, Cassandra emphasized *political engagement* for students in most of her responses to the questions, which she viewed as distinct from or in tension with "practicality" and *teaching for transfer* to other writing courses in the university (which was a significant motivation for Samantha and other instructors across multiple focus groups).

LaFrance writes that a writing program is "always a site of contestation, disorder, divergence, and disagreement—created in the interactive tensions between what are loosely related sets of individual practices that live below official, institutional, and professional discourse" (113). This kind of institutional ethnographic analysis provides writing program administrators with a way of exploring these tensions, and it also shows how the focus groups themselves are performances of individual and programmatic identity. Through these conversations, participants were able to articulate their values and practices in collaboration with others. Their negotiations were made public to the other participants, and the collaborative nature of the focus group may have helped instructors to articulate tensions and resistances that they experience as well.

CONCLUSION

Moments of true resistance, where instructors completely rejected the values or practices espoused by the writing program, were rare in the focus groups for this project. This isn't surprising in itself—the nature of the study, where instructors came together with me, a graduate student administrator, for an unpaid focus group meeting, shaped the types of responses they were likely to share. Instructors who were passively resistant to the values of the writing program, perhaps viewing their teaching not as part of their own identity but as something that helped to finance their "real work" as graduate students, were unlikely to participate in the first place. But tensions and ambivalences, where instructors had difficulties or "mixed feelings" about their work, appeared frequently in our conversations. In her discussion of the work of "linked courses," LaFrance explains that "even empowered and aware individuals must work within the co-constituted contexts of their sites," and therefore "[m]oments of resistance and divergence, even when significant in the slow processes of long-term change, are often invisible to all but a small handful of people" (68). Within the framework of institutional ethnography, focus groups offer opportunities to make these "moments of resistance and divergence" public and visible to other members of the writing program. Sharing these moments with each other in the space of the focus group is important in itself, but analysis of these moments also provides researchers and WPAs perspective on the ways that resistance is often mediated by institutional ruling relations that shape teachers' experiences of their work.

Institutional ethnography allows us to recast resistance and difference as natural processes within any workplace and gives us the means to uncover the lines of power and ruling relations that organize these resistances. I want to suggest that resistance, especially resistance to change in a writing program, is not merely stubbornness or inflexibility, but rather comes about from disjunctures in the roles that instructors play in the institution and the values that accompany those roles. The instructors' experiences that I have presented in this chapter suggest that invisible aspects of their work (such as emotional labor) may create tension for instructors in fulfilling the expressed values of the writing program. As LaFrance reminds us in the Introduction and Chapter 1 of this volume, institutional ethnography allows researchers to reconceptualize work to include the often-invisible labor that surrounds negotiating emotions, values, and identities, both individual and collective, through the material lived experiences of people in institutions. Doing so allows researchers, WPAs, and instructors to understand, acknowledge, and co-create more sustainable programs that make space for ambivalence and resistance. IE also allows us to see how deeply held values from other aspects of their embodied or disciplinary identities inform the ways that instructors interact with and take up their work in the teaching of writing. Rather than simply resisting resistance, we can create spaces for discussion and negotiation of the programm's collective identity while still listening to and privileging the experiences and values that instructors bring. By slowly uncovering what is happening in our programs and institutions, IE may also allow us to work toward creating space for all members of the writing program to retain agency in the ways that negotiate their individual teaching identities as they work together toward a shared enterprise in the writing program.

WORKS CITED

Burnham, Christopher, and Susanne Green. "WPAs and Identity: Sounding the Depths." *The Writing Program Interrupted: Making Space for Critical Discourse*, edited by Donna Strickland and Jeanne Gunner, Boynton/Cook Publishers, 2009, pp. 175–85.

Dryer, Dylan B. "The Persistence of Institutional Memory: Genre Uptake and Program Reform." *WPA: Writing Program Administration*, vol. 31, no. 3, 2008, pp. 32–51.

Ebest, Sally Barr. *Changing the Way We Teach: Writing and Resistance in the Training of Teaching Assistants.* Southern Illinois UP, 2005.

Framework for Information Literacy for Higher Education. American Library Association, 2 Feb. 2015, http://www.ala.org/acrl/standards/ilframework.

Framework for Success in Postsecondary Writing. Council of Writing Program Administrators (CWPA), the National Council of Teachers of English (NCTE), and the National Writing Project (NWP), 2011, https://files.eric.ed.gov/fulltext/ED51 6360.pdf.

Griffith, Alison I., and Dorothy E. Smith. "Introduction." *Under New Public Management: Institutional Ethnographies of Changing Front-Line Work*, edited by Alison I. Griffith and Dorothy E. Smith, University of Toronto Press, 2014, pp. 3–22.

Grouling, Jennifer. "Resistance and Identity Formation: The Journey of the Graduate Student-Teacher." *Composition Forum*, vol. 32, Fall 2015. https://compositionforum .com/issue/32/resistance.php.

Hollander, Jocelyn A. "The Social Contexts of Focus Groups." *Journal of Contemporary Ethnography*, vol. 33, no. 5, Oct. 2004, pp. 602–37. https://doi.org/10.1177 /0891241604266988.

LaFrance, Michelle. *Institutional Ethnography: A Theory of Practice for Writing Studies Researchers*. Utah State UP, 2019.

Restaino, Jessica. *First Semester: Graduate Students, Teaching Writing, and the Challenge of Middle Ground*. Southern Illinois UP, 2012.

Smith, Dorothy E. *Institutional Ethnography: A Sociology for People*. AltaMira Press, 2005.

———. "Texts and the Ontology of Organizations and Institutions." *Studies in Cultures, Organizations and Societies*, vol. 7, no. 2, Jan. 2001, pp. 159–98. https://doi .org/10.1080/10245280108523557.

Wilkinson, Sue. "Focus Groups: A Feminist Method." *Psychology of Women Quarterly*, vol. 23, no. 2, June 1999, pp. 221–44. https://doi.org/10.1111/j.1471-6402.1999. tb00355.x.

"Writing Across Technology Overview." First-Year Writing. University of Connecticut. http://fyw.uconn.edu/resources-for-instructors/writing-across-technology/. Accessed 13 Mar. 2019.

PART THREE. EXPANDING UNDERSTANDINGS OF INSTITUTIONAL COORDINATION

CHAPTER 5.

WRITING STANDPOINT(S): INSTITUTION, DISCOURSE, AND METHOD

Erin Workman
DePaul University

Madeline Crozier
University of Tennessee, Knoxville

Peter Vandenberg
DePaul University

The chapter before you is not what we envisioned when we began drafting it in early 2020, just before we began to experience the radical spatial disjuncture delivered by the global pandemic. The pandemic disrupted not only our ongoing longitudinal research on conceptions of writing circulating within our institution but also our site of study and every aspect of our lives and those of our participants. What we imagined to be a straightforward continuation of our ongoing institutional ethnography (IE) quickly morphed as the "COVID-19 discourse" (Luken 2) rewrote and recalibrated local and translocal relationships in ways we could not have anticipated; however, as this chapter demonstrates, IE is helping us to see and make sense of these disrupted and shifting relations by "opening up new and different analytic windows, as well as opportunities for activism and change" (Spiner and Comber 253), specifically within our first-year writing (FYW) curriculum and professional development initiatives.

Taking up Michelle LaFrance and Melissa Nicolas' call for "more institutional ethnographies in our field" ("Institutional Ethnography" 145), we initially framed our multi-stage project as one intended to uncover what, where, and how *writing* means for varied stakeholders at our institution, DePaul University (DPU), a mid-sized, private, Catholic university in the Midwest. Inspired by LaFrance's study "on the circulation of *information literacy* as a key term" in her FYW program (105), we began a similar inquiry on *writing*, first focusing on institutional sites known for their attention to writing—the writing center and our independent writing department—and eventually expanding our exploration to university sites

DOI: https://doi.org/10.37514/PER-B.2023.2029.2.05

where the activity of writing facilitates, but is not understood as, *work*. We aimed to make visible university stakeholders' conceptions of writing as they "circulated through the many ways of doing, knowing, and being that constituted" our university (LaFrance, "An Institutional Ethnography" 108) and, like Cristyn Elder (this volume), to map where on campus undergraduate writing is valued and supported. Unforeseeably, IE would only become more crucially significant to us, as writing researchers, to acutely recognize the "disjunctions and erasures" (LaFrance, *Institutional Ethnography* 73) of work processes and social relations made manifold by the COVID-19 pandemic. While our research questions have remained consistent over the four years of our study, our research site, and our individual positions in relation to it, has changed. Having found other preliminary reports on ongoing IE projects (e.g., Eastwood; LaFrance and Nicolas, "What's Your Frequency?") instructive for our own, we hope that our readers will likewise find value in our reflections on how the methodology continues to reshape our understanding of the problematics that we set out to explore.

This chapter begins with a description of our research design and modifications we made as the project progressed. It then illustrates how we have recursively analyzed our data to identify "sites of interface between individuals and a vast network of institutional relations, discourses, and work processes" (McCoy 111), foregrounding how disruptions surfaced by the pandemic have revealed to us the unstable and co-constitutive nature of standpoint and ruling relations. As we trace the *work processes* mapped in our study (i.e., how people's work is organized and coordinated by their activation of texts), and what these processes reveal about writing at DPU, we argue that writing is not only a vehicle for work processes, but *is* work in many institutional sites, whether stakeholders recognize it as such or not (see Miller, this volume, for a discussion of writing as work). Although the claim that writing is work appears self-evident for writing centers and departments, the processes by which that work is continuously coordinated and co-accomplished in "micro-moments" as individuals interface with institutional discourses and ruling relations are not always visible or evident, especially as these processes and practices become so routinized as to be just *how things are done*. After addressing limitations and implications of our study for the everyday work of writing at DPU, we conclude by reflecting on opportunities for action emerging through this research.

RESEARCH DESIGN: STANDPOINT(S), PROBLEMATICS, AND METHODS

Our project arose from the situated, temporally oriented perspectives of the three contributing researchers: Erin, a newly hired assistant professor and incoming

FYW Director hoping, like LaFrance, to "gain[] important understandings of the complex program" she would soon direct ("An Institutional Ethnography" 106); Pete, founding chair of our independent writing department seeking to understand how and why writing instruction faded from its privileged role in strategic planning efforts of the mid-00s; and Madeline, a master's student and writing tutor interested in exploring the motivations and purposes behind local writing center practices. Given our distinct yet overlapping interests, we took up IE for its systematic, foundational concepts through which to analyze relationships between individual practices and experiences and the social and institutional forces that continuously reshape, and are reshaped by, those practices. Central to our interests, the heuristics of *standpoint, work, work processes,* and *ruling relations* guided our research design and data analysis across all stages of our project.

Data collection and analysis have spanned four years to date and unfolded across three stages, each focused on differently positioned stakeholders in various university sites, though, as we came to realize and will address below, the stability and uniformity of institutional categories, which subsume individual standpoints, work against the aims of IE. Because institutions are "site[s] of dialogic and multivocal belongings," institutional ethnographers often begin their studies with surveys and interviews "to get a sense of the 'language, thinking, concepts, beliefs and ideologies' that constitute a site" (LaFrance, "Institutional Ethnography, *Handbook*" 461, 467), a process that we likewise followed. Although we modified protocols to account for varied particularities of context across individuals, all participants were asked to define writing and discuss influences shaping that definition; they also discussed their writing practices and work processes when speaking, for example, about specific texts or in relation to their job description(s). These questions prompted participants to reflect on the extent to which their conceptions of writing (re)shape, and are (re)shaped by, their institutional position(s) and daily work processes. As the following sections will illustrate, the flexibility of IE, along with our project's development across three stages, has afforded us opportunities to refine research protocols along the way to bring into focus the "micro-moments" in which university stakeholders "actively negotiate their belongings within institutional locations" (LaFrance, "Introduction," this collection).

STAGE I: CO-CONSTITUTIVE PERCEPTIONS OF WRITING AND WORK IN THE WRITING CENTER

Our research began in May 2018 with an IRB-approved pilot project in the writing center (WC), the central program of the University Center for Writing-based Learning (UCWbL) within the Office of Academic Affairs.[1] Like the

---

1   IRB protocol #MC051718LAS.

study conducted by Michelle Miley and her team (this collection) our inquiry began in the WC and then branched out to closely interconnected sites. Because IE "begins in the reality of work experience," the methodology guided us to ask how tutors' "understanding and experience of their work coordinates with the work of the writing center and how the actuality of that work shapes our understanding" (Miley, "Looking Up" 109). Beginning with tutors' standpoints to "look up" at how their work is textually mediated by boss texts inscribing ruling relations, Madeline, from her position as a member of the WC's research and assessment team, distributed a survey to her fellow tutors, asking about their conceptions of writing and writing practices in relation to their perceptions of the work of tutoring (for a similarly focused faculty survey, see Nugent et al., this collection). Understanding that "texts create the essential connection between the local of our bodily being and the translocal organization of ruling relations" (Smith 119), Madeline also conducted discourse-based interviews (see Crozier and Workman; Odell et al.) with tutors, using their self-selected written feedback samples from recent tutoring appointments to ground discussions of practice while staying attuned to "the situated variability of experience within institutions" that give rise to different practices (LaFrance and Nicolas, "Institutional Ethnography" 133). These discourse-based interviews helped us to elicit tutors' knowledge about the work of writing and to trace their activation of boss texts—such as the tutoring handbook and UCWbL mission, values and beliefs—in their written feedback.

To identify standpoints and trace work processes, we read data for hooks and traces of institutional discourses and moments "where discourse and the particularities of lived experience refuse[d] and resist[ed] one another" (LaFrance, *Institutional Ethnography* 39–40). We came to realize, like LaFrance and Nicolas before us, the difficulty of "[a]ttempting to account for various standpoints in the writing center community" given "variations in job descriptions and related work practices" ("What's Your Frequency?" 11). Although our participating WC administrators shared the same HR classification of *full-time professional staff*, participating tutors ranged from undergraduate and graduate students with various disciplinary and departmental affiliations to long-term professional staff, some of whom also teach part-time for FYW. Tutors across these institutionally designated categories also held WC leadership positions or, like Madeline, contributed to one or more "teams;" consequently, tutors' work knowledges and processes vary considerably depending on the "two or three" roles they elect to "take on" (UCWbL 21).

For example, two participants sharing the institutional category of *graduate assistants* articulated different understandings of WC work contoured by the particularities of their additional roles, which they held for equal lengths of time.

Participant C, assisting the multilingual writing team, defined WC work as "providing a sense of community" for "a student who is coming from another country," emphasizing that the WC should be "a home away from home," a place where tutors make "them feel like they're part of the community." Participant E, serving on the workshops team and as a writing fellow and WC receptionist, understood WC work as "supporting writers in any stage of the writing process, in any discipline, and for any genre" and made no reference to multilingual writers or linguistic diversity. Just as these participants conceptualized WC work differently, so too did they offer different definitions of writing, with participant C emphasizing that writing can be defined from "multiple perspectives" and participant E defining writing as "expressing your ideas through written form." By drilling down into the nexus of roles and positions subsumed by institutional categories, which imply uniformity and stability not reflective of embodied practice, we began to see how tutors' standpoints, definitions of writing, and perceptions of WC work co-evolve as they routinely activate organizational texts "for another first time" with each tutoring appointment (Dippre 73).

STAGE II: INSTITUTIONALLY CAPTURING WRITING IN THE WRITING STUDIES DEPARTMENT

Struck by the ways in which institutional categories subsumed individuals and WC discourse regulated variations in standpoint, we chose to focus the second stage of our project on the majors and minors in the Department of Writing, Rhetoric & Discourse (WRD). We were curious about the variations we were certain to find between boss texts—catalog content, course descriptions, learning outcomes, and so on—and students' individualized uptake of the programs' efforts to regulate and authorize particular understandings of *writing* and related practices in alignment with the ruling relations and disciplinary discourses of writing studies. By extending our inquiry into our department as a point of relation to the WC, we also hoped to develop a better understanding of "the effects of the coordination between the two," especially given their independence from one another (Miley, "Mapping" 76). Thus, in May 2019, after refining the survey instrument and discourse-based interview protocol to focus on WRD and participants' self-sclected meaningful writing projects (Eodice et al.), Madeline distributed the survey using the department's student mailing list and conducted interviews with survey respondents who opted in.[2]

In keeping with the disciplinary orientation of our department, we were not surprised to find that participants identified themselves as writers across

---

2   IRB Protocol #MC041819LAS.

contexts, though we found the variation in participants' talk about writing quite striking. While some used department language to define writing as "a system of communication" or anything where "symbols [are] produced visually," a few participants, who defined writing as *expression* and emphasized the actions writing can accomplish, pulled from their lived experiences across lifeworlds while also illustrating how they were acculturating to and resisting professional and disciplinary discourses. Pete, from his perspective as founding department chair, expressed dismay that some WC tutors—lacking substantial coursework in rhetoric and writing theory taken by WRD majors and minors—displayed vocabulary that seemed to better control (or be better controlled by) disciplinary threshold concepts. As we studied department texts, such as website copy and course descriptions, we came to see that although explicit discussions about writing occur in all WRD courses, there are no boss texts like those Jim Nugent et al. (this collection) describe that are purposely intended to motivate a shared conceptual vocabulary—such as those mediating the work of tutors in the WC. While syllabus policies and course descriptions may *intend* such an outcome, lacking the WC's cohort structure and boss texts, they do so only implicitly and therefore less influentially.

Examining this disjuncture by way of IE led us to a crucial insight about our tacit expectations that WRD majors and minors would define writing in terms of writing studies threshold concepts (Adler-Kassner and Wardle). Attuned to the importance of researcher reflexivity, Pete and Erin considered how their standpoints as unit- and program-level administrators shaped their valuation of expressive conceptions of writing, rendering them more susceptible to *institutional capture*, defined by Dorothy Smith as "a discursive practice, regulated by the institutional procedures of text-reader conversations through which institutional discourse overrides and reconstructs experiential talk and writing" (119). Because their managerial roles required them to enact ruling relations inscribed in disciplinary texts (e.g., Adler-Kassner and Wardle; CWPA) and to routinely create and activate institutional texts (e.g., WRD Dept. Bylaws, FYW Faculty Handbook, Syllabus Checklist, Term Faculty Observation Form) to render individual practices accountable within *institutional circuits*, Pete and Erin came to see how key terms they understood to be shared across the department—including *writing*—actually "len[t] an illusory sense of pedagogical connection to national and professional discussions of writing pedagogy" (LaFrance, "An Institutional Ethnography" 107). As we will discuss when considering the implications of our study, this disjuncture between ideals of practice and individuals' actual material practices opened space for us to consider and "initiate productive and lasting interventions" to our writing curricula (LaFrance "Introduction," this collection).

STAGE III: WRITING AS WORK IN ACADEMIC
AND CO-CURRICULAR UNIVERSITY SITES

Up to this point of our study, we assumed a relatively stable institutional field across our three stages of inquiry, having no way to anticipate a global pandemic that would quite literally dis-orient our participants and ourselves, dramatically altering our embodied experiences of institutional work and the ruling relations coordinating that work translocally. Virus mitigation measures necessarily reoriented our relationship to each other and to our participants in several crucial ways: we modified interview protocols to include questions about the effects of remote work on writing processes; we conducted all interviews via Zoom, an adjustment enabling Pete and Erin to co-conduct more interviews with administrators and staff than would have been possible given travel between DPU's Lincoln Park and Loop campuses; and, although we did not initially plan to interview staff members, we came to see the value of doing so early in our Stage III data collection and, thus, revised our IRB protocol[3] to include staff members whose position descriptions entailed communication with various stakeholders.

When we began interviewing participants in early April 2020, it became clear that the context of COVID-19 created significant "difference, divergence, and disjunction within sites of writing" that revealed disruptions in some, but not all, participants' work processes (LaFrance, *Institutional Ethnography* 71). As we discuss in the next section, these disruptions surfaced previously hidden social relations and habitual practices that, ironically, became visible only in their suddenly notable absence. No matter the extent to which digital technologies may have already been mediating institutional relations locally and extralocally, the sudden collision of competing discursive values and habits as work and home came to overlap decidedly altered both the work of writing and how we would continue our project of tracing this work.

TRACING THE WORK OF WRITING
IN A GLOBAL PANDEMIC

In our WC and WRD stages, participants sometimes struggled to describe in detail their writing and work processes, but this difficulty disappeared with our Stage III participants who were concurrently grappling with disruptions to their typical work processes and able to consciously reflect on practices that would typically fly below the radar. For instance, as norms and conventions for institutional email correspondence gave way to quickly emerging and pressing

---

3   IRB Protocol #EW020320LAS-R3.

exigencies, participants had to reconfigure their approach to this ubiquitous genre in ways that rhetorically addressed the gravity of the current moment and considered readers' decreasing bandwidth as emails came to replace what would typically be face-to-face conversations. As one newly appointed department chair noted during her April 18 interview:

> I found that all of us have come up with a thousand new ways to say, *I hope all is well.* Every email is a variation on *how are you?* Then the final, the salutation . . . at the end is also *be well,* some variation of that, too. I think we're embedding in our writing to each other these well wishes, or trying to voice some kind of concern, and also acknowledge the insanity of this moment. You [Pete] and I even exchanged some emails about this, about how weird it is to be doing business when there are cooler trucks with dead people in them. It's just crazy. There's such a cognitive dissonance, sort of, that you're like making a D2L quiz, and you can't go outside. (Participant 14)

The emotional labor of "coming up with a thousand new ways" to embed care and well wishes into emails that have, conventionally, avoided such expressions, emerged across administrator and staff interviews and was further amplified by the recognition that words could not repair the cognitive dissonance of going about business as usual while infection and death rates were growing exponentially worldwide, with "alarmingly disproportionate rates" in Black and Latinx communities in Chicago and across the U.S. (Corley, para. 1).

Focused on ways to stay connected with and support students—especially those who are multiply marginalized or unhoused—in their routine and emergent needs, the coordinator of a support center in Student Affairs described the work of creating various channels in Microsoft Teams to direct "students who have needs for food [to the] Dean [of student]'s office or places where they can find food," like DPU's food pantry, or "to help students with books because . . . there's no longer inter-library loans" (Participant 209). Although the coordinator acknowledged that "Teams has been essential to make sure we're not . . . dropping the ball for any of our students who need us," he also admitted that "it's information overload. I'm not gonna lie. It can be a bit intimidating, and sometimes I just have to log off 'cause I'm just like, 'Okay, I can't keep up with all this information coming from everywhere.'" Recognizing the need to quickly pivot from campus-based outreach to digitally-mediated outreach, this coordinator described how writing—and reading—became the focal work of his office. As LaFrance observes, "how people are positioned within a site will often dramatically impact not only what people do but how they do it" (*Institutional Ethnography* 110). When "the site" becomes exclusively virtual, altered material conditions produce functional changes with both material and ontological implications.

Many participants *felt* these functional changes in relation to the impact of physical space on their writing and work processes. From a librarian to the many students who, having previously relied on writing in the library and on campus, found themselves affected by the disruption of working remotely, struggling to develop new work processes and maintain "professionalism" in spaces that were typically *not* used for DPU work.

> **University Librarian 213:** I've got this [gestures to] china cabinet behind me and I don't have an office at home, but I have an office at work. And I have a system where I put different things on different post-it notes and move them around and I don't—I mean, I suppose I could do that [here, on the china cabinet], but I haven't found my legs yet for that.

> **First-Year Student 305:** I was writing this [philosophy essay] at my childhood home with my grandma walking in, asking me if I want apple slices and stuff. I feel like being at home definitely adds a different context to it where it's like . . . *I still feel like a child here* because I'm at my house rather than an apartment or something. [It] takes away the professionalism to me.

For stakeholders like this librarian and student, whose work routinely takes place on campus, the shift to working remotely required additional material resources and labor that remained invisible to those faculty and administrators for whom remote work was already typical, such as faculty in the College of Business where online, asynchronous courses have long been a standard part of the curriculum.

> **Associate Professor of Business 404:** [L]argely what I've been doing for the past 10, 15 years is working remotely. I find that if I go into the university for anything but teaching or a scheduled meeting, if I'm in my office *it descends into gossip*. People come by and they want to chat and want to fool around. If I want to get stuff done, I work here at my home office. I've designed an ergonomic space that I've had for 25 years, and it just totally rocks for me. I've got everything I need.

Interestingly, what this well-resourced associate professor refers to as "gossip" was understood differently by faculty-administrators and staff who routinely work both on and off campus and came to recognize, in their absence, how integral those moments of stopping by to chat were for their (seemingly isolated) work processes.

Almost overnight, teleconferencing modalities reconstituted not only the material interface between stakeholders, but their potential for interaction. We saw this most decidedly in our administrator and staff participants' discussions of working to create new processes for collaboration and connection. No longer able to "just go next door to talk to somebody" (Dean 23), some administrators and staff realized the importance of happenstance interactions, now conspicuously absent, and created virtual spaces to encourage and mediate the informal social connections essential to maintaining communities of practice.

> **Associate Provost (AP) 12:** *I hadn't realized so keenly until now* how much intel you're just picking up standing reheating your lunch or walking down the hall or *in the women's room now that we have a lady provost.* Little bits of stuff you pick up here and there that then when you get back to your desk, have helped you understand how better to say something in order to be heard. . . . I've been missing that kind of just *unscripted, incidental,* intelligence of the community.

> **Vice President (VP) 10:** Something that has come up in the last few weeks, obviously, the new normal, whatever we want to call it—DPU 1.5—while we're in this *temporary* mode, we've really been trying to think about community, and how do we keep our community strong while we can't be physically close to each other? And so, there's a tool we rolled out for the institution called Microsoft Teams that's sort of got a social component to it, and we've really pushed this [in Information Services (IS)]. So, we created a space—we call it IS-tagram, like playing on Instagram. I'm just trying to get people to share pet photos, just anything, little comedic things you found in the news today.

Analyzing these moments through the IE concept of *standpoint*, which "recognizes that we are implicated in social networks in ways that may not always be entirely clear," we see in these participants' talk about *work processes* the invisible social relations that come into view when routine processes are interrupted (LaFrance, *Institutional Ethnography* 95). AP 12, in referring to conversations that take place "in the women's room now that we have a lady provost," reveals a recent shift in social relations that afforded administrators using the women's room private access to the provost—access that, presumably, was previously afforded to administrators using the men's room. Because these encounters happen behind closed doors, the co-constitutive work of writing is erased, resulting in texts understood by both author and reader(s) as the work of one person. In the absence of physical proximity, what VP 10 likened to a "spiderweb that you can feel the threads being pulled" on by others, many stakeholders came to recognize the degree to which their work had always been co-constituted, acknowledging how integral these incidental conversations are to how the work of writing—and of the university—comes to happen as it does.

REFLECTING ON THE IMPLICATIONS OF WRITING AS WORK

As we acknowledge above, ongoing analytical work has revealed limitations in our multi-stage research design. By tightly circumscribing each stage and site, we initially "look[ed] at each individual site as unique," precluding the possibility of seeing "the effects of the coordination" among the WC, WRD, and various university sites (Miley, "Mapping" 76). Likewise, our reliance on institutional categories for identifying and recruiting participants prevented us from seeing how unique standpoints are subsumed by these categories: WC tutors are undergraduate and graduate students—in some cases, WRD majors, minors, MA students, and alumni—and they are also part-time instructors for FYW; administrators with various disciplinary and professional identifications also hold faculty and staff positions; and staff, some of whom are also WRD MA alumni, are integral to the work of writing at all levels of the university, from (re)designing curricula for the career center to coordinating professional development opportunities for faculty, from serving as instructional designers to teaching part-time and piloting new modalities for FYW. Looking only from the macro perspective of organizational charts, one could easily surmise that the work of writing is limited to those university units claiming it as their subject.

However, as we were reminded through the process of reanalyzing WRD data, even in these sites where writing explicitly organizes work knowledge and processes, what *writing* means varies just as much, if not more so, than in other university sites. When confronted with our devaluation of expressive conceptions of writing and our tacit expectations that WRD participants would discuss writing by way of disciplinary threshold concepts, we traced this ideological position to ruling relations inscribed in disciplinary texts like the WPA Outcomes Statement (CWPA), which has been critiqued for "enact[ing] Eurocentric epistemological perspectives" that "inflict covert racial violence by marginalizing the linguistic epistemologies of raciolinguistically minoritized students" (Kareem 28) and reinscribing "race evasive" discourses (Kynard 166); excluding "African American rhetorics, Native American rhetorics, Chicano/Chicana rhetorics, Asian American rhetorics, and queer rhetorics just to name a few" (Carter-Tod, para. 13); and perpetuating habits of white language supremacy (Inoue) and anti-Black linguistic racism (Baker-Bell). As Carmen Kynard, Staci Perryman-Clark, Sheila Carter-Tod, Vershawn Ashanti Young and Michelle Bachelor Robinson, and many other Black, Indigenous, Latinx, and scholars of color have been arguing for the duration of our field's existence, incorporating African American and cultural rhetorics into writing curricula and professional statements offering ideals of practice—like the WPA-OS—is imperative for cultivating antiracist and inclusive programs and courses, countering linguistic racism, and "helping students understand, analyze, and produce based on a broader concept of knowledge of rhetoric(s)" (Carter-Tod, para. 19). Extending similar critiques to *Naming What We Know*, Tessa Brown argues that excluding "creative writers' knowledge," as Pete and Erin were inclined to do, further "limit[s] contributions and theorizations from writers of color" (607). Surfacing this problematic, then, helped to reveal "whose interests are served," or not, through local instantiations of recommended best practices (Campbell and Gregor 15).

Through IE, we can see how what appeared to be an unquestioned disciplinary value for non-expressive conceptions of writing actually has more pernicious consequences for social justice and equity. As Marie Campbell and Frances Gregor remind us, "[n]ot understanding an organization is one form of domination. Understanding it and having it shape a course of action is another" (15). Uncovering this problematic opened up new lines of inquiry, enabling us to explicate these differently valued conceptions of writing, and provided an exigence for revising our FYW curriculum to be inclusive of and attentive to non-Eurocentric epistemological perspectives (Kareem), literacies, cultural rhetorics, and rhetorical traditions beyond the "Aristotelian rhetorical model" (Carter-Tod, para. 11)—a project already underway through FYW's development of a custom, student-facing textbook like that described by Nugent et al. (this volume). In combination with a modified "disparate impact analysis" of student learning outcomes (Poe et al.) and a new professional development initiative for FYW faculty, program-wide adoption of the *DPU Guide to Meaningful and Transformative Writing* (Workman, Hohenzy, and MacKenna-Sandhir) in Fall 2022 will, hopefully, prompt students and faculty alike to reflect on and expand their conceptions and valuations of writing.

Despite the limitations of our research design, we hope, like Elder (this volume), that continuing to trace writing across our university will contribute to "a more accurate map . . . that spans a much wider territory and offers a more layered landscape," one that we already see coming into view through our ongoing IE project and related programmatic initiatives (Miley, "Looking Up" 124). We hope that this map will offer us a "means of creating a culture of writing and a recognition of interdependence within our institution," especially as we work toward linguistic justice and antiracist practices (Miley, "Mapping Boundedness" 77).

CONCLUSION: MAKING SENSE OF EMERGENT RULING RELATIONS

We began our study intending to uncover "the routine textual work [that] puts together [our] large-scale institution and its outcomes" so that we could render visible the complex of institutional discourses and ruling relations mediating various stakeholders' work processes (Turner 139). Now in November 2022, over four years later, we find our IE project in a state similar to most other aspects of our lives; it has been disrupted in ways we could not have anticipated, and while this disruption has surfaced tacit work knowledges, revealed co-constitutive writing and work processes, and opened up space for critical intervention in FYW, its trajectory seems inevitably moving toward problematics we can scarcely predict. As the perceptions of disruption articulated above reveal, some of the situated textual activities that give rise to "replicable forms of social action," which, for Turner, "*are* the acts *of* the institution" (140), have lost definition in the institutional architecture. Others are emergent, but far from mundane, routinized, or standardized.

While IE positions us to locate and investigate a "temporal sequence of activities that is coordinated, recognizable, and reproducible" (Turner 148), more visible at the moment we revise this manuscript are ripples traveling through the ruling relations. Even as DPU transitioned most stakeholders back to campus in the 2021–2022 academic year, both quickly emergent exigencies and routine committee meetings *still* call out for teleconferencing, and the weakened temporal constraints associated with face-to-face orders of interaction continue to disrupt the familiar textual order—circumstances will no longer wait, for example, on the leisurely meeting schedule written into Faculty Council bylaws. The capacity to launch meetings with fewer material constraints, for some, makes possible new affinities, alliances, and working relationships unimaginable when this study began, though, by the same token, stakeholders without material and technological resources to participate in these conversations are excluded. The "architectural significance" of some boss texts, as mechanisms of social control, have been lessened as familiar conditions of material organization are replaced by these other measures of coordination. Robert's Rules of Order never saw the Zoom Chat functionality coming.

In these uncertain conditions, we push forward with our project, assured that where routinized prescriptive texts or sequenced textual practices are losing shape or giving way, the methodology of institutional ethnography will continue to offer a means for understanding how the work of writing comes to happen as it does and opening spaces for activism and change.

ACKNOWLEDGMENTS

The authors would like to thank the DePaul University Research Council and the College of Liberal Arts and Social Sciences for their generous funding of this project, and co-researcher Deyana Atanasova, who joined the project for Stage III. We also express our gratitude to the 99 DPU stakeholders who shared their experiences as participants in this project.

WORKS CITED

Adler-Kassner, Linda, and Elizabeth Wardle, editors. *Naming What We Know: Threshold Concepts of Writing Studies*. Utah State UP, 2015.

Baker-Bell, April. *Linguistic Justice: Black Language, Literacy, Identity, and Pedagogy*. Routledge, 2020.

Brown, Tessa. "What Else Do We Know? Translingualism and the History of SRTOL as Threshold Concepts in Our Field." *College Composition and Communication*, vol. 71, no. 4, 2020, pp. 591–619.

Campbell, Marie, and Frances Gregor. "Analyzing Data in Institutional Ethnography." *Mapping Social Relations: A Primer in Doing Institutional Ethnography*, edited by Marie Campbell and Frances Gregor, University of Toronto Press, 2002, pp. 83–101.

Carter-Tod, Sheila. "Rhetoric(s): A Broader Definition." *Composition Studies FEN Blog*, 29 Mar. 2021, https://compstudiesjournal.com/2021/03/29/rhetorics-a-broader -definition/.

Corley, Cheryl. "Chicago Tackles COVID-19 Disparities in Hard-Hit Black and Latino Neighborhoods." *NPR WBEZ Chicago*, 9 June 2020, https://npr.org/2020 /06/09/869074151/chicago-tackles-covid-19-disparities-in-hard-hit-black-and -latino-neighborhoods.

Crozier, Madeline, and Erin Workman. "Discourse-Based Interviews in Institutional Ethnography: Uncovering the Tacit Knowledge of Peer Tutors in the Writing Center." *Composition Forum*, vol. 49, 2022, https://compositionforum.com/issue/49 /institutional-ethnography.php.

CWPA. "WPA Outcomes Statement for First-Year Composition (3.0)." Council of Writing Program Administrators, 17 Jul. 2014. https://wpacouncil.org/aws/CWPA /pt/sd/news_article/243055/_PARENT/layout_details/false.

Dippre, Ryan J. *Talk, Tools, and Texts: A Logic-in-Use for Studying Lifespan Literate Action Development.* The WAC Clearinghouse / UP of Colorado, 2019. https://doi.org/10.37514/PRA-B.2019.0384.

Eastwood, Lauren. "Making the Institution Ethnographically Accessible: UN Document Production and the Transformation of Experience." *Institutional Ethnography as Practice*, edited by Dorothy E. Smith, Rowman & Littlefield Publishers, 2006, pp. 109–25.

Eodice, Michelle, et al. *The Meaningful Writing Project: Learning, Teaching, and Writing in Higher Education.* Utah State UP, 2016.

Inoue, Asao. *Above the Well: An Antiracist Literacy Argument from a Boy of Color.* The WAC Clearinghouse / UP of Colorado, 2021. https://doi.org/10.37514/PER-B.2021.1244.

Kareem, Jamila M. "Covert Racial Violence in National High-School-to-College Writing Transition Outcomes." *Violence in the Work of Composition: Recognizing, Intervening, Ameliorating*, edited by Scott Gage and Kristie S. Fleckenstein, Utah State UP, 2022, pp. 28–44.

Kynard, Carmen. *Vernacular Insurrections: Race, Black Protest, and the New Century in Composition-Literacies Studies.* SUNY Press, 2013.

LaFrance, Michelle. "An Institutional Ethnography of Information Literacy Instruction: Key Terms, Local/Material Contexts, and Instructional Practice." *WPA: Writing Program Administration*, vol. 39, no. 2, 2016, pp. 105–23.

———. "Institutional Ethnography." *Handbook of Research Methods in Health Social Sciences*, edited by Pranee Liamputtong, Springer Nature, 2019, pp. 457–70.

———. *Institutional Ethnography: A Theory of Practice for Writing Studies Researchers.* Utah State UP, 2019.

LaFrance, Michelle, and Melissa Nicolas. "Institutional Ethnography as Materialist Framework for Writing Program Research and the Faculty-Staff Work Standpoints Project." *College Composition and Communication*, vol. 64, no. 1, 2012, pp. 130–50.

———. "What's Your Frequency?: Preliminary Results of A Survey on Faculty and Staff Perspectives on Writing Center Work." *The Writing Lab Newsletter*, vol. 37, no. 5–6, 2013, pp. 10–13.

Luken, Paul C. "Institutional Ethnography: Sociology for Today." *The Palgrave Handbook of Institutional Ethnography*, edited by Paul C. Luken and Suzanne Vaughan, Palgrave Macmillan, 2021, pp. 1–8.

McCoy, Liza. "Keeping the Institution in View: Working with Interview Accounts of Everyday Experience." *Institutional Ethnography as Practice*, edited by Dorothy E. Smith, Rowman & Littlefield Publishers, 2006, pp. 109–25.

Miley, Michelle. "Looking Up: Mapping Writing Center Work through Institutional Ethnography." *The Writing Center Journal*, vol. 36, no. 1, 2017, pp. 103–29.

———. "Mapping Boundedness and Articulating Interdependence Between Writing Centers and Writing Programs. *Praxis: A Writing Center Journal*, vol. 16, no. 1, 2018, pp. 75–87.

Odell, Lee, et al. "The Discourse-Based Interview: A Procedure for Exploring the Tacit Knowledge of Writers in Nonacademic Settings." *Research on Writing: Principles and Methods*, edited by Peter Mosenthal et al., Longman, 1983, pp. 221–36.

Perryman-Clark, Staci. *Afrocentric Teacher-Research: Rethinking Appropriateness and Inclusion*. Peter Lang, 2013.

Poe, Mya, et al. "The Legal and the Local: Using Disparate Impact Analysis to Understand the Consequences of Writing Assessment." *College Composition and Communication*, vol. 65, no. 4, 2014, pp. 588–611.

Smith, Dorothy E. *Institutional Ethnography: A Sociology for People*. AltaMira Press, 2005.

Spiner, Nerida, and Barbara Comber. "Transnational Power Relations in Education: How It Works Down South." *The Palgrave Handbook of Institutional Ethnography*, edited by Paul C. Luken and Suzanne Vaughan, Palgrave Macmillan, 2021, pp. 237–58.

Turner, Susan Marie. "Mapping Institutions as Work and Texts." In *Institutional Ethnography as Practice*, edited by Dorothy E. Smith, Rowman & Littlefield Publishers, 2006, pp. 139–61.

UCWbL. *How to UCWbL: The Handbook*. University Center for Writing-based Learning, DePaul University, 2017.

Workman, Erin, Victoria Hohenzy, and Erin MacKenna-Sandhir. *DePaul University Guide to Meaningful & Transformative Writing*. Fountainhead Press, 2022.

Young, Vershawn Ashanti, and Michelle Bachelor Robinson. "Introduction: African American Rhetoric: What It Be, What It Do." *The Routledge Reader of African American Rhetoric: The Longue Dureé of Black Voices*, edited by Vershawn Ashanti Young and Michelle Bachelor Robinson, Routledge, 2018, pp. 3–8.

CHAPTER 6.

"WRITING ISN'T JUST WRITING": AN INSTITUTIONAL ETHNOGRAPHY APPROACH TO THE WORK OF COMMUNITY WRITING CENTER INSTRUCTORS

Elisabeth Miller

University of Nevada, Reno

Madison Writing Assistance (MWA) is a community writing program initiated in 1999 at the University of Wisconsin, Madison. Originally named "Community Writing Assistance," this grant-funded program provides one-on-one writing assistance to individuals across the city of Madison at public libraries and community centers. Over the past 20-plus years, MWA has grown from one public library site staffed by volunteer graduate students staked out with the sign, "Writing help here!" to an average of eight community sites staffed by paid graduate-student instructors each semester and summer. MWA has come to mean many things to stakeholders: instructors (usually Ph.D.s in rhet/comp or literature, or MFAs in creative writing) call it, as a recent testimonial from a MWA grant proposal reveals, one of the "most meaningful, impactful, and important" parts of their graduate education. Community partners value it for supporting writing, basic computer skills, and employment needs. UW-Madison calls it an important outreach program.

In this essay, I contend that institutional ethnography (IE) is an especially useful methodological lens for building knowledge about a program like MWA, which is uniquely situated between two overlapping institutions: a large public, land-grant mission research university and a mid-size midwestern metropolis—between a university and a community. Analyzing survey responses from current and former MWA instructors as well as program materials, I (a former MWA instructor and administrator) show how taking an IE approach to studying the work experiences and perspectives of MWA instructors expands our knowledge about 1) the tensions that often arise in community and university partnerships, and 2) the work of community writing instructors—contributing to the broader

DOI: https://doi.org/10.37514/PER-B.2023.2029.2.06

theory and practice of community literacy programming (Doggart et al.; Grabill; Rousculp). As Patrick Berry writes in his study of prison education programs, while instructors often describe community-focused teaching as the most influential experiences of their professional lives, little attention is paid to their perspectives. It is imperative, Berry argues, to account for instructors' perspectives to avoid falling into the damaging tendency to view community-based literacy instruction as "one-sized and selfless," acknowledging that "the last thing we need is another story of the teacher as savior" (68).

These kinds of knowledge gaps arise, Michelle LaFrance argues, as writing studies "has often been preoccupied with narratives of program design, curriculum development, and management—discourses that tend to standardize, generalize, and even erase the identities, expertise, and labor contributed by diverse participants" (7). An IE approach, instead, "offers a comprehensive and situated means to uncover all the highly specific and individualized ways in which work actually takes shape within institutional settings" (7)—including, in this collection, WAC programs (Elder), first-year writing programs (Nugent et al.), and research focus groups (Book), among other diverse sites. To gather—and "look up" from—instructor perspectives, I emailed a survey to 59 current and former CWA/MWA writing instructors. 30 responded to the survey, a 51% response rate.[1] I decided to ask questions in the form of an open-ended survey for two reasons. I wanted to allow instructors 1) to participate at their own pace, taking the time they needed to answer questions, at their convenience; and 2) to participate anonymously. I wanted to ensure open and honest responses, and I also wanted to encourage both those who did not know me (I worked in instructor and administrative positions with the MWA program for five-and-a-half years) and those who did to share their experiences, without being concerned with revealing their identities to me. I also distributed a short survey to current MWA partners, and I reviewed program documents, including grant proposals from the last five years and website materials from MWA and UW-Madison.

I designed the brief surveys to take an IE approach (see the Appendix). Sociologist Dorothy Smith laid the groundwork for IE as "a method that" first "followed from taking up women's/people's standpoint in the local actualities of the everyday;" not just of "discovering the everyday world as such, but of looking out beyond the everyday to discover how it came to happen as it does" ("Introduction" 3). In this way, IE traces social phenomena in "the experiences of specific individuals whose everyday activities are in some way hooked into, shaped by, and constituent of the institutional relations under exploration" ("Introduction" 18). To attempt to trace these institutional relations in the work

---

1   IRB approved study.

of community writing center instructors, I asked participants to define the mission and work of MWA, to elaborate on concrete experiences with the program, to comment on how they perceive the program's value for the community and for themselves as professionals. In this way, I take up the "orienting concept" of "work" from IE approaches (McCoy 110), which Smith defines as "what people do that requires some effort, that they mean to do, and that involves some required competence" (*The Everyday* 165). In this framing, "work happens at (gears into) the interface between the individual, embodied subject and the physical and social worlds" (McCoy 111).

In what follows, I use IE approaches to interrogate what the "work" of community writing centers means to the instructors who engage in it, "making visible the values, practices, beliefs, and belongings that circulate below more visible or dominant discourses" (LaFrance 5). Specifically, I identify a boss text, and ruling relation, for MWA: "The Wisconsin Idea," a kind of university mission that seeks to expand the "boundaries" of the university to the surrounding community and beyond. I then show how the Wisconsin Idea, while it suggests community and university overlap, in fact conflicts with 1) the standpoint of current and former MWA instructors, particularly their understanding of tensions between the community and university, and 2) other boss texts and ruling relations that guide "writing center" best practices—including non-directive approaches. These conflicts expose how community and university are in fact not synonymous, but rather, are often in tension, and how attempts to import the values of the university into "the community" are, in fact, not social justice. I close by demonstrating how an IE approach to work helps build knowledge of "writing as work" that learns from the on-the-ground experiences of community writers and writing instructors.

"THE WISCONSIN IDEA" AS BOSS TEXT AND RULING RELATION

"The Wisconsin Idea" is a philosophy, tagline, and ruling relation at the University of Wisconsin—Madison focused on how the "boundaries of the university are the boundaries of the state." Originally credited to the first UW-Madison president Charles Van Hise in 1903, the Wisconsin Idea university still uses this mission today to frame itself as a land-grant institution committed to public engagement, with its website describing the idea as "[o]ne of the longest and deepest traditions surrounding the University of Wisconsin," "signif[ying] a general principle: that education should influence people's lives beyond the boundaries of the classroom." The idea, the website claims, has been "synonymous with Wisconsin for more than a century," a "guiding philosophy of university outreach efforts in Wisconsin and throughout the world." In an IE approach, the Wisconsin Idea can be understood as a boss text: a term originated (Griffith and Smith 12) "to acknowledge that some texts exert a powerful material and local influence over the everyday work lives of professionals" (LaFrance 80). LaFrance explains how "boss texts" "regulate—and often standardize—practice, mediating idiosyncrasies and variability in local settings" (43).

Though it is not explicitly articulated in MWA's mission or program materials, the Wisconsin Idea permeates the language instructors use to describe the program. Nine of the 30 survey respondents directly refer to the Wisconsin Idea. Seven of those nine occur in response to the question, "How would you describe your understanding of the mission of the MWA/CWA program?" MWA is "a textbook illustration of the Wisconsin idea. Applying a skillset typically limited to academic work to the large population of writers elsewhere in Madison," one responds. Another explains that they have "often heard it referenced in relation to the Wisconsin Idea—the concept that the university exists to serve the broader community and region." Two others define MWA as "an extension of the UW-Madison writing center," an example of how to enact the Wisconsin Idea, which they define as "The walls of the classroom are the walls of the state."

Shaping how MWA instructors talk about and interpret their work, the Wisconsin Idea operates as boss text and as a "ruling relation." As Smith clarifies, ruling relations are "extraordinary yet ordinary:" ("Introduction" 8) what LaFrance explains as "powerful social and workplace norms" that "draw upon and influence institutional patterns, such as hierarchies, allocations of resources, and work processes" (32). These relations become invisible insofar as they can be understood as "just how it's done," but they in fact "coordinate and/or organize daily experiences and practices, influencing what people do and how they do it across space and time" (32). That kind of tacit uptake of the Wisconsin Idea is apparent in MWA instructors' responses. Beyond explicit naming, respondents use related language invoking a link or bridge between community and university: "My understanding of the mission," one instructor explains, "is that it seeks to bridge community-university divide by offering free writing instruction to community members on any project they may bring." Likewise, other instructors use the "broader" and "beyond" language of the Wisconsin Idea: MWA, other instructors assert, "exists to serve the broader community and region," "to make the best knowledge and practice of one-to-one writing instruction to writers beyond the University." This outreach mission characterizes the Wisconsin Idea—"benefiting" and "serving" the community: MWA, instructors claim, aims "to help build partnerships between the university and the surrounding community in order to use university resources for the benefit of the community," and "to serve the writing needs of the Madison community."

COMPLICATING "THE WISCONSIN IDEA": MWA INSTRUCTORS' CONFLICTING STANDPOINTS, BOSS TEXTS, AND RULING RELATIONS

While the influence of the Wisconsin Idea as a boss text and ruling relation for MWA is apparent, an IE analysis of instructors' survey responses reveals how community writing instructors' on-the-ground work, and perspectives on that work, conflict with and complicate the Wisconsin Idea's easy conflation of university and community. First, I show how instructors grapple with tensions between community and university—and how they identify as belonging, or not belonging, in either location. Second, I interrogate how tensions between the boss text and ruling relation of "good writing center pedagogy" complicates the Wisconsin Idea's call for simply "extending" into the community.

1) INSTRUCTOR STANDPOINTS: COMMUNITY AND UNIVERSITY DISCONNECTS

As LaFrance notes, while "ruling relations enable institutional ethnographers to trace broad social patterns, 'standpoint' helps the ethnographer to uncover the disjunctions, divergences, and distinctions experienced by individuals within those groups" (35). Survey responses reveal how the Wisconsin Idea is challenged by examining MWA instructors' standpoints—particularly their sense of how community and university often conflict. While they are members of the university, instructors' description of their work in MWA reveals a more complex relationship between university and community than the Wisconsin Idea's "extending of the university into the community" accounts for. Several instructors identify a sense not of "extension" or blending between "university" and "community," but rather of a "community-university divide." Drawing a clear boundary-line between their experiences inside and outside of the university, five respondents use the terms "campus bubble," "UW bubble," "academic bubble," and "grad school bubble." "It is easy to stay in the campus bubble," one writes, and community writing instruction "helped me to feel more connected to the Madison community."

In addition to the spatial metaphor of an academic "bubble" and getting outside of that bubble that appears in instructors' responses, four instructors referred to tensions between community and university in their own experience of being graduate students. After saying that they "hoped" that the MWA program "would support social justice by partners [sic] with members of the local community and helping them reach their own goals," one instructor refers specifically to their own family's "blue collar background": "both my parents were first generation college students. Sometime working in the university felt distant from my own background, and I wanted the benefits of my field and of my own education to reach my uncles, my cousins, my grandparents—and those with similar literacies." Another straightforwardly acknowledges, "I needed to be outside of the space of Helen C. White (the English building), and frankly enjoyed the walk to the Library and enjoyed being with the people I met there. It felt very familiar."

Feelings of familiarity or distance, associations with walking in neighborhoods, invocations of family, or not fitting at the university, frame the way instructors explain their decisions to participate in MWA. Describing the benefits of MWA, one instructor notes how it provided "a break from school, a break from the research university. I never felt like I belonged at an R1 and MWA was one of the things that helped me make it through the program." Another sums up the physical and metaphorical spaces and gaps between university and community, citing MWA as "a connection to the university—right up the street, but so inaccessible."

2) Boss Texts in Conflict: The Wisconsin Idea, Writing Center Best Practices—and Beyond

In addition to disconnects in instructors' standpoints, an IE analysis of instructors' responses also exposes a tension between the boss text and ruling relations of the Wisconsin Idea and the boss texts and ruling relations of writing center pedagogy and practices. As the community-based arm of a university writing center, MWA employs the one-to-one talking-about-writing model that characterizes best practice in academic writing centers. Most of MWA's staff have completed writing center training and served as academic writing tutors for some time. As instructors describe teaching in the MWA program, they note how writing Center pedagogical principles and strategies are sometimes inadequate, even inappropriate, for the support desired and required by community writers.

DIRECTIVE/NON-DIRECTIVE METHODS

Many MWA instructors refer to and challenge some of the most foundational ruling relations in writing center practice: particularly directive vs. nondirective methods and the emphasis on the writer versus the writing product. The most commonly cited framing of these writing center "ruling relations" can be traced to Stephen North's boss text for writing center studies: "The Idea of a Writing Center." In that piece, North claims that "[o]ur job" in writing centers "is to produce better writers, not better writing" (483). That is, writing centers should focus on the student, not the paper; on process, not product. Tutoring methods should avoid "appropriating" writers' ideas by not being too "direc-tive" and should, instead, focus on a writers' growth in ways they can take on to their next assignment (Brooks). While writing center scholarship (Shamoon and Burns) has substantially complicated any facile divide between "directive" and "non-directive," the responses of many MWA instructors demonstrate how nondirective methods may be insufficient for community contexts—even less liberatory than they have been imagined in university writing center approaches.

One instructor reflects at length about the "pretty big disconnects" they observe between writing center "pedagogical training" and "some of the flexi-bility and savvy required to consult with community members." "For instance," they go on, "I feel like in my training, non-directiveness was celebrated as an aspirational tutoring value—especially as it was positioned in binary terms against 'directiveness,' which was positioned as having more to do with con-trol, authority, and not valuing what a writer wanted." However, at MWA, they "found that non-directive and facilitative orientations to tutoring often didn't work when applied with writers who were struggling to cultivate genre expertise, technological literacies, or maybe just wanted to hear advice from someone they felt 'knew more about writing than them.'"

When asked to describe "one or two vivid memories of working with the CWA/MWA program (a patron, a project, etc.), this instructor elaborates on the second session they ever conducted and the fraught results of their "taking a really non-directive approach, asking a lot of facilitative and open-ended ques-tions." The instructor recalls that

> this approach totally didn't work with this writer. To most of my questions, he said, "I'm not sure. That's why I'm ask-ing you, as an expert." And that totally threw me for a loop because, for the most part, the sort of dialogic, question-pos-ing style of tutoring I'd used was fairly successful with uni-versity students. And so I recall, from this point on, thinking to myself, "Maybe what I know about tutoring writing, and what I've done so far isn't quite going to cut it in different settings when there are different stakes what with this person's personal/job/life situation."

In this MWA instructor's on-the-ground work, the boss text/ruling rela-tion endorsement of "non-directive," "process v. product-focused" instruction comes into crisis as they wonder if what they "know about tutoring writing" is insufficient for a community writing context. Instructors like this one describe how the work of community writing—with its "different stakes" focused on jobs and life situations, and with community members looking for "expert" support—pushes back on the Wisconsin Idea's aim to simply "extend" the university to the community. Here, university writing center methods fail to "cut it." Rather, working with MWA "taught" them, one instructor noted, "that meeting students where they were often meant leaving behind 'best practices' or the ongoing emphasis on process not product. When a person needs a cover letter for a job, they need a product."

Likewise, the urgency of the writing situation—often a job application to acquire vital work—changed the teaching context: "we had very little time to teach everything the partner [patron, client] needed to know about the genre, stylistic expectations, grammatical expectations, computer skills, etc. We taught the most critical ones, but the goal there, as explained to me by the organization, was a product (usable job materials in little time), not a long, slow learning process." Producing a "paper" like a resume or cover letter in one hour, for instance, may be more important than gaining and refining genre knowledge of resumes over several sessions. Or put another way: that hour may be the only option for time, and that literate product (or lack of it) has a very immediate material consequence. While the boss text/ruling relation of the Wisconsin Idea advocates for extending the boundaries of the university to the boundaries of the community, state—even globally—it does not necessarily provide context or tools for what happens there: how should university-based knowledges, methods, ways of communicating be employed? Translated? Shifted? Rejected? As the reflections of MWA instructors reveal, university-based writing center best practices, such as non-directive tutoring methods, cannot merely be "extended" into community contexts.

THE BOUNDARIES OF COMMUNITY WRITING INSTRUCTION

As with instructors' reflections on belonging (or not) in the university and the community, the in-between-ness of community writing center work also arises from its situatedness between institutions. In these in-between contexts of community writing, an IE analysis helps us to understand how the boss text/ruling relations of university writing centers—focusing on a non-directive, process approach—may be inadequate for addressing the needs of community writers. In response, a question recurs throughout instructors' efforts to define their work: what, exactly, is inside (and outside) the bounds of community writing center instruction? Advertising for MWA (like university writing centers) invites community members to bring in any writing—of any genre, at any stage—that they are working on. However, the range of genres and rhetorical contexts community writers face proves to be quite wide. In addition to methods and best practices coming under pressure, the very roles of instructor and student/patron/writer are unsettled in community contexts. As one instructor observes, "Academia is constructed to minimize the ambiguity of the relationship between any two people working together in an academic setting. Much of the apparatus of the writing center—the scheduling infrastructure, the physical details of the site—was built to replicate something like the dentist/patient relationship." "MWA interactions," the instructor observes, are "much more ambiguous: writers were sometimes just looking for an audience who would listen to them or who would stamp an approval of their work, or they were mistrustful of my feedback and advice no matter how carefully I (thought I) couched it. I'm not sure I ever learned to negotiate the ambiguity of that relationship." This ambiguity in MWA instructors' roles arises, in part, out of the failure of boss texts/ruling relations of the Wisconsin Idea and university-based writing center best practices to guide and support community writing center work. In turn, MWA instructors are left grappling with what methods for writing support they should develop and deploy, how to adapt to a range of (often high-stakes) genres, and how to negotiate their role as community writing instructors.

Several instructors reflect on the methods for instruction they develop in community contexts. "It was nothing like typical writing center work," one instructor explains of working with one of MWA's longest-running patrons—a woman writing her medical memoirs: "Basically, she told us stories and asked us to transcribe them. Since she came back every week, I got to know her very well and learned a lot from her about small town and farm life in the upper Midwest. Mostly, she needed an enthusiastic, curious listener who could help draw out more of her stories." Another instructor shares a memory of a regular patron who "would bring with him each week a sheaf of lined looseleaf paper, covered from top to bottom with the man's handwriting, usually in pencil. He would talk for an hour or so with great energy and apprehension about his project. Never once did he show me a single page of writing."

Others reflect on dealing with unfamiliar genres. One recalls "working with a woman who was writing a letter to a lawyer to ask for help to appeal her sister's conviction of some kind" and being "in WAY over my head, but somehow we corralled a nearby library patron who was a retired lawyer (I think?) to help us and eventually the three of us all had our hands on the keyboard almost writing together—and then one of the writer's kids also came over and sat in her lap." These complex, high-stakes writing tasks, and their often substantial demands for genre knowledge, require being "super resourceful and fast" or, says the instructor who shared the experience of the appeal letter, "okay with floundering or saying I just didn't know." "We didn't always know the genres that people were working with," one instructor reflects, "and something I knew I wasn't the one the person should be consulting. With that, I also understood that I might have been their only option." MWA instructors identify both urgent demands (sometimes long lines for especially job-focused writing support and a feeling of "pressure to move through them quickly") and scarcity of resources to support community members. The combination of pressure and sometimes ambiguous expectations further stresses these interactions. Patrons may bring unrealistic expectations, says one instructor, that MWA staff "will spontaneously know how to write or phrase something perfectly and that's particularly challenging. It can be difficult to set clear expectations about we can do as instructors."

Likewise, the ambiguity of instructors' roles further complicates navigating new genres and interactions. One instructor notes the complexity, for instance, of handling "professional moments with people who are older than me, making sure they don't stay over time and things like that." Another reflects on an "unpleasant experience" working with a patron who questioned her "ethnic position," asking "questions about 'where I am from' or talk about 'I know another person from X country' instead of engaging with writing. It was a tricky situation because I didn't know how to establish good boundaries and I didn't feel like the authority in the room (compared to how I feel as a TA in a classroom)." These moments make especially vivid how both the Wisconsin Idea and some university-based writing center best practices (as boss texts/ruling relations) fail to offer on-the-ground strategies and support for community writing instructors.

"WRITING AS WORK" AND "WORK AS WRITING" IN A COMMUNITY WRITING CENTER

Using IE to analyze the work of MWA instructors provides a powerful way to interrogate how boss texts and ruling relations like the Wisconsin Idea and writing center best practices (despite their best intentions) that circulate in universities may fail to account for—or even conflict with—community contexts. I close by discussing the value of an alternative ruling relation that emerges from instructors' reflections on their work as community writing center instructors, from MWA program materials, and from an IE approach to "work": that writing is work, and work is writing. (See Miley in this volume for a similar discussion of how research conducted by undergraduate tutors build their knowledge of a kind of "thirdspace" of the work of writing centers).

Analyzing MWA's grant proposals over the last five years reveals a "ruling relation" in MWA's mission "to help Madison-area residents use the written word to live rich and productive lives:" a focus on writing as doing, writing in use, or writing as work. Taken from a librarian at the longest-running MWA location, one quotation that recurs across MWA's grant proposals reinforces this ruling relation: "People are hard at work trying to live their lives as responsible citizens, workers, students, business people, helpers, and neighbors," the librarian writes. "MWA recognizes that 'ordinary' people have a need to communicate information in a host of different ways and need help doing it. MWA helps to do this hard work better." In this framing, writing is work, and work is writing, and it is the work of community writing instructors to support the work of everyday writers. As Deborah Brandt argues in her tracing of the divergent histories of reading and writing, while reading has been linked with moral and religious instruction, writing has long been tied up with work. Writing *is* work.

MWA instructors' responses support this perspective on writing as work (and their work to support it). One instructor observes how MWA has revealed to them "all the different ways in which people use literacies in their everyday lives from legal documents, to religious websites, to personal narratives, to children's books to job materials." Another instructor notes how they "became aware of a much wider range of literacy activities that people take part in, and how big a role literacy plays in their lives in so many different ways. So it widened my perspective on what it means to teach writing and in what diverse contexts writing matters." Practically speaking, another instructor says the experience they gained supporting a range of writers and writing projects "provided me with a lot of writing consulting/teaching credibility. For years, I felt I could say 'Yes, I've worked on that kind of document, or something like that,' about almost anything, from cookbooks to professional websites to business plans"—a very useful set of experiences as this instructor went on to a Ph.D. program in rhetoric and writing studies.

In addition to building their flexibility and knowledge as teachers, the experience of supporting writers and their work exposed for instructors "A broadened definition of writing! I also learned about how members of the community actually use writing to advocate for themselves and for their cause." The ways that writing is work and is wrapped up in people's lives with getting work done is articulately expressed by one instructor:

> I think my work with community members in MWA helped me understand writing isn't just writing: inscription of words onto a page or screen. So much of what I did was help participants navigate legal forms, local and state agencies, learn computer software/hardware, and more. In a real-world sense, MWA helped me understand how everyday people navigate a range of texts, infrastructures, and institutions.

An understanding of writing as work learns from how "writing isn't just writing"—but a tool for "navigating" legal, technological, economic aspects of the institutions we work within every day. The work of community writing center instructors, then, is about supporting that navigation.

IMPLICATIONS FOR PRACTICE & THEORY

In closing, I want to briefly highlight how a ruling relation of "writing as work" pushes back on both the Wisconsin Idea and writing center boss texts/ruling relations and the ways they reduce both instructors' backgrounds and perspectives and community writers' complex literacy contexts and needs.

1) TRAINING & SUPPORTING INSTRUCTORS

My IE analysis of instructors' description of their work in MWA reveals the boss texts and ruling relations of the Wisconsin Idea and of university writing center best practices fail to account for the complexity of the work on the ground of MWA—potentially limiting both instructors and writers. Instructors' reflections on their own backgrounds are more complex than a "university" affiliation reveals. Rather than conflating the two as the Wisconsin Idea does, community writing centers would do well to acknowledge how the backgrounds that instructors bring with them to community writing instruction are valuable assets, and including space for reflections on instructors' own (dis)connections to communities or to the university.

Similarly, the genres and needs of community writers are not the same as those that commonly appear in university writing centers. The time-intensive nature of resumes, the high stakes of documents such as immigration paperwork or legal appeals or even life memoirs, and the ways that such genres are often tied to bureaucracy, all create challenges for instructors. These factors in community writing necessitate, as instructors reflect, a "broadened definition of writing" as more than "just writing," that must be addressed in training community writing instructors, as examples from practice, challenging scenarios, and shared insights from experienced instructors can be productively shared. Ambiguous roles, too, in programs that blend university and community, highlight the need for increased support from both institutions. It is essential to address both the patrons' and the instructors' comfort and safety: for instance, MWA has begun having patrons sign forms agreeing to conduct and to limited use of sessions, and on-site support from librarians or community center staff is absolutely invaluable.

2) THEORIZING COMMUNITY LITERACY
PROGRAMS THROUGH IE

I reiterate here Smith's "generous conception" of work in IE as "what people do that requires some effort, that they mean to do, and that involves some required competence" (*The Everyday* 165). As Timothy Diamond finds in his IE study of nursing assistants, much of the work people do is not officially "charted," and IE research encourages us to identify and theorize about "about work where we didn't think it existed" (50). Analyzing the work of community writing instructors yields a similar finding: that writing is work, not only insofar as it supports vocations, but as in the IE definition of making something happen, of putting effort in. As already evident in MWA program framing, a notion of work—and writing as work—is a powerful argument for the mission and value of community literacy programming. Literacy educators, researchers, and program advocates have long grappled with the complexity of making arguments for our programs that do not resort to literacy myth and literacy crisis logics (Branch; Street). While aligning literacy with an IE conception of "work" does not eliminate these thorny problems, it does, I argue, contribute untapped insights from the on-the-ground work and standpoints of community writing instructors. These insights expose how university (such as the Wisconsin Idea) and field-wide (such as writing center best practices) boss texts and ruling relations may fail to account for the realities of community writing and community writing instruction. Uncritically extending the ruling relations of universities into communities risks failing to serve, and further marginalizing, community writers.

IE offers a particularly powerful method to literacy researchers' efforts push back on this marginalization by generating a finer-grained articulation of the centrality of writing and literate activity to the institutions we navigate everyday—from immigration processes and webs of documents (Vieira) to infrastructures such as "government and commerce" (Vee 51) to the economies we inhabit (Brandt). As Jeffrey Grabill claims, "institutions give literacies existence, meaning, and value"—and both literacy and institutions cannot be understood apart from one another (7). Taking an IE approach to the work of community writing instructors, I have aimed to contribute to those efforts: highlighting how boss texts and ruling relations may oversimplify and, ultimately, hold back community/university connections—including instructors and writers. Taking an IE approach, the "work" of MWA instructors is far more complex: influenced by instructors' backgrounds and sense of belonging (or not), challenged by the ways writing center pedagogies do (or do not) translate to community contexts, and defined by "writing as work."

WORKS CITED

Berry, Patrick. *Doing Time, Writing Lives: Refiguring Literacy and Higher Education in Prison*. Southern Illinois University P, 2017.

Branch, Kirk. "Literacy Hope and the Violence of Literacy: A Bind That Ties Us." *College English*, vol. 79, no. 4, 2017, pp. 407–20.

Brandt, Deborah. *The Rise of Writing: Redefining Mass Literacy*. Cambridge UP, 2015.

Brooks, Jeff. "Minimalist Tutoring: Making the Student Do All the Work." *Writing Lab Newsletter,* vol. 15, no. 6, 1991, pp. 1–4. https://www.wlnjournal.org/archives /v15/15-6.pdf.

Diamond, Timothy. "'Where Did You Get the Fur Coat, Fern?' Participant Observation in Institutional Ethnography." *Institutional Ethnography as Practice,* edited by Dorothy Smith. Rowman & Littlefield, 2006, pp. 45–64.

Doggart, Julia, et al. "Minding the Gap: Realizing Our Ideal Community Writing Center." *Community Literacy Journal,* vol. 1, no. 2, 2007, pp. 71–80.

Grabill, Jeffrey T., 2001. *Community Literacy Programs and the Politics of Change.* State University of New York P, 2001.

Griffith, Alison I., and Dorothy E. Smith. *Under New Public Management: Institutional Ethnographies of Changing Front-Line Work.* University of Toronto P, 2014.

LaFrance, Michelle. *Institutional Ethnography: A Theory of Practice for Writing Studies Researchers.* Utah State UP, 2019.

McCoy, Liza. "Keeping the Institution in View: Working with Interview Accounts of Everyday Experience." *Institutional Ethnography as Practice,* edited by Dorothy Smith. Rowan & Littlefield, 2006, pp. 109–26.

North, Stephen M. "The Idea of a Writing Center." *College English,* vol. 46, no. 5, 1984, pp. 433–46.

Rousculp, Tiffany. *Rhetoric of Respect: Recognizing Change at a Community Writing Center.* NCTE, 2014.

Shamoon, Linda K., and Deborah H. Burns. "A Critique of Pure Tutoring." *Writing Center Journal,* vol. 15, no. 2, 1995, pp. 134–51.

Smith, Dorothy. *The Everyday World as Problematic: A Feminist Sociology.* Northeastern University P, 1987.

———. "Introduction." *Institutional Ethnography as Practice,* edited by Dorothy Smith. Rowman & Littlefield, 2006, pp. 1–12.

Street, Brian. *Literacy in Theory and Practice.* Cambridge UP, 1984.

Vee, Annette. "Understanding Computer Programming as a Literacy." *Literacy in Composition Studies,* vol. 1, no. 2, 2013, pp. 42–64.

Vieira, Kate. *American by Paper: How Documents Matter in Immigrant Literacy.* University of Minnesota P, 2016.

"The Wisconsin Idea." *University of Madison Wisconsin.* https://www.wisc.edu /wisconsin-idea/. 2020.

APPENDIX. CWA/MWA INSTRUCTOR SURVEY QUESTIONS

1. What year did you graduate (or do you expect to graduate) from UW-Madison?
2. What program are/were you enrolled in?
3. What is your current occupation?
4. How many terms (counting semesters and summers) did you work with the Community Writing Assistance/Madison Writing Assistance program?

5. At which MWA/CWA sites do/did you work?
6. What led you to decide to work with CWA/MWA?
7. How would you describe your understanding of the mission of the CWA/MWA program?
8. Describe one or two vivid memories of working with the CWA/MWA program (a patron, a project, etc.).
9. What would you describe as the primary benefits to you of participating in CWA/MWA?
10. What would you describe as the primary benefits to the community/community members of the CWA/MWA program?
11. What was most challenging about working with the CWA/MWA program? What, if anything, helped with those challenges (or could have helped)?
12. How, if at all, has working with CWA/MWA influenced you as a professional?
13. How, if at all, has working with CWA/MWA influenced you as a person?
14. Are there any other aspects of your work with the CWA/MWA program—experiences, benefits, challenges—that you wish to address?

CHAPTER 7.

FROM A FACULTY STANDPOINT: ASSESSING WITH IE A SUSTAINABLE COMMITMENT TO WAC AT A MINORITY-SERVING INSTITUTION

Cristyn L. Elder

University of New Mexico

Spring 2018 marked the start of a two-and-a-half-year "probationary" period I was given to set up a writing across the curriculum (WAC) program at the University of New Mexico (UNM)—probationary because we had just been through three different provosts, some interim, in the past three years, and the final say on the establishment of a WAC program would be given to the next (and, hopefully, longer-lasting) provost once hired. Prior to this period, UNM did not have a formal WAC program, nothing beyond the singular efforts of individual faculty, a handful of graduate students, or a lone disciplinary program. With my background and research interests squarely in writing program administration, and WAC specifically, I saw this as a great opportunity to serve both faculty and students in the creation of a sustainable WAC program to support the further development of students as writers across the disciplines at UNM.

My immediate goal as UNM's first WAC director was to learn more about my campus as a ready site for WAC. This initial step, *understanding the institutional landscape,* as Michelle Cox et al. have named it, is the first stage of the whole systems approach to sustainable WAC[1] and consists of the following three strategies: 1) *determining the campus mood,* 2) *understanding the system in order to focus on points of interactivity and leverage,* and 3) *understanding the ideologies that inform the campus culture of writing* (64–66). Forefront on my mind was the question, then, of how my institutional context would shape, or *contour* as

---

1   Cox, et al.'s whole systems approach to sustainable WAC consists of four stages: 1) Understanding the Institutional Landscape, 2) Planning a Program, 3) Developing Projects and Making Reforms, and 4) Leading for Sustainability.

DOI: https://doi.org/10.37514/PER-B.2023.2029.2.07

Michelle LaFrance so aptly puts it, the conceptions of writing (and perhaps of writers) found at UNM ("Institutional" 28). In an effort to address this question, I adopted a number of heuristics from institutional ethnography (IE) as a materialist framework, which both shaped my methodology and influenced my analysis of the data collected, as described below. But, first, I describe the unique institutional context that is UNM.

INSTITUTIONAL RESEARCH CONTEXT

UNM is the state of New Mexico's flagship university. The Albuquerque campus, where I am located and where this research took place, is a Hispanic-Serving Institution and the only Carnegie-classified "very high research" R1 institution in the state. In Fall 2019 (pre-COVID-19), of the 21,498 students on campus, over 87% (18,671) were from the state of New Mexico ("Fall 2019" 16), and over 70% of beginning freshman who had recently graduated from a New Mexico high school were students of color (19).[2] Additionally, nearly half of UNM's undergraduate student population identifies as "first generation," with neither parent having received education beyond high school or not having earned a four-year degree ("First Gen Proud"). At UNM, we often proudly say we teach the future demographic of higher education—today.

As for the larger context in which UNM is situated, year after year, and again in 2019, the state of New Mexico ranked the lowest in child well-being (50th state out of 50), including in terms of overall health (48th), economics (49th), family and community (50th), and education (50th). While the Annie E. Casey Foundation reported an improvement on average across the US in 11 of the 16 "Kids Count" index measures for child well-being,[3] they also reported that, as a nation, we "have failed to eliminate the racial and ethnic inequalities" that continue to leave many children and their families behind (9). This is perhaps nowhere more apparent than in the state of New Mexico, based on the above measures.

IE: A MATERIALIST FRAMEWORK

In *Institutional Ethnography: A Theory of Practice for Writing Studies Researchers*, La France explains that "[t]o undertake an IE project is to uncover the empirical

2 For Fall 2019, the percentage by race/ethnicity at UNM of beginning freshmen who recently graduated from New Mexico high schools was reported as follows: 60% Hispanic, 24% White, 5% Asian, 4% American Indian, 4% Two or More Races, 1.7% Black or African American, .5% Non-U.S. Resident, .7% Race/Ethnicity Unknown, and .1% Native Hawaiian ("Fall 2019").
3 For the "16 Key Indicators of Child Well-Being by Domain," see The Annie E. Casey Foundation's 2019 Kids Count Data Book: State Trends in Child Well-Being, pp. 12–15.

connections between writing as individual practice and the conditions that make a site of study unique" (18). That is, our distinctive institutional contexts shape our teaching and learning practices as well as our attitudes about writing and writers, whether explicitly or invisibly. IE can help uncover how and why this interplay happens by revealing how the work of an individual is influenced by the material conditions and the work of others within the university. UNM, the site of my IE research, represents one of only a handful of Hispanic-Serving R1 Institutions in the US and enrolls a significant percentage of undergraduate students from traditionally marginalized and excluded backgrounds who now represent one of the fastest growing demographics in higher education. With this student demographic, and the austerity challenges the state of New Mexico faces, UNM offers a rich landscape for examining through the lens of IE how the material actualities of a public institution influence the teaching and learning of students and campus readiness for WAC.

As I set out to do this research, I adopted the IE heuristic approach of a *standpoint*—specifically that of faculty across the disciplines at UNM (Rankin, "Conducting . . . Analytical Work"). This faculty standpoint is the empirical location from which I collected data on the workings of the university and its relationship to undergraduate writing instruction across disciplinary courses, curriculums, schools, and colleges on campus. As Janet Rankin explains, standpoint informants understand their work "ideologically," or in theoretical terms of what is supposed to happen (e.g., faculty's understanding of best pedagogical practices), and "materially," or in empirical terms of what really happens (e.g., how those best practices manifest in the classroom in response to institutional forces) ("Conducting . . . Analytical Work" 2).[4] It is from a faculty standpoint, then, that my research questions originated:

1. How much interest is there among faculty across the disciplines for WAC?
2. What faculty ideologies about writing (and undergraduate writers) might help or hinder the development of sustainable WAC at UNM?
3. What material aspects may support or challenge faculty's work in supporting undergraduate writers across the disciplines?

Furthermore, this faculty standpoint informed the data collection tools I developed for the mixed-methods approach I took to address these questions, resulting in a faculty survey; semi-structured faculty interviews; and the collection of teaching artifacts, including course syllabi, assignment prompts, and writing assessment criteria.[5]

---

4   In this edited collection, Miley, et al. helpfully refer to this as the "ideal" versus the "real," in their examination of a third space where the ideal and the real might find alignment.

5   University of New Mexico IRB study #14829.

Determining the Campus Mood

As Cox, et al. argue, determining campus mood is an important aspect of assessing the overall readiness of an institution's commitment to student writing across the curriculum. Measuring this readiness includes "a mix of collecting data, talking to stakeholders, reflecting on current writing practices across university contexts, and identifying points of conflict and support concerning possible WAC program models" (87). To assess the campus mood at UNM, beginning from a faculty standpoint, I distributed a 35-item survey to 1,300 individual faculty in the fall of 2020 on UNM's Albuquerque campus. Due to space, however, I limit my focus in this chapter to the following two survey items:

- What are your motivations for having students write in [a chosen] course?
- What are your challenges or the barriers for you having students write in [a chosen] course?

I paired these two questions specifically as I believed the first to likely reveal *theoretical* reasons for faculty integration of student writing in their courses across the disciplines and the second to uncover *material* aspects either encouraging and/or inhibiting that work.

Despite the difficult semester faced at the time of this research, brought on by a global pandemic, I was encouraged by the 344 participant responses (26%) to the survey, from which I isolated responses to the two questions above. Of the total participants, 226 faculty (86%) reported positively to integrating writing into at least one undergraduate course, with these courses representing every college or school on UNM's Albuquerque campus with an undergraduate degree program. While not definitive, this wide-ranging, positive response from faculty across the disciplines bodes well for identifying a coalition of faculty supportive of discussions about WAC on campus. This "baseline" understanding of faculty mood can be useful for examining how favorable conditions might be for introducing new WAC approaches within UNM's curricular ecology before, as Cox, et al. suggest, allocating more time and resources to WAC interventions (89).

Identifying Points of Interactivity and Leverage

Beyond determining mood, Cox, et al. additionally recommend identifying points of interactivity and leverage for bringing about transformational change to one's institutional context. It is at these points that one may begin to see "pathways of least resistance" within the complex institutional system for sustainable approaches to WAC. From the IE faculty standpoint I have adopted, these points include where within the institution faculty are focused on writing and writing outcomes across their curricular contexts. These faculty points of entry can help identify "what interventions should be made, at what levels, in what order, and on what scales" as well as help determine which initiatives should be prioritized "to have greatest impact/leverage and simultaneously achieve maximum buy-in" (90–91). The responses from faculty in this study suggest multiple pathways within all disciplines for building and strengthening writing support across the curriculum.

UNDERSTANDING IDEOLOGIES INFORMING THE CAMPUS CULTURE OF WRITING

For a more complete ethnography of writing across the curriculum within an institution, it is necessary to not only analyze the mood of campus stakeholders such as faculty and the places within the larger network where writing is taking place but to also understand the ideologies about writing that underlie the pedagogical ecology of the institution that may support (or obstruct) the development of a formal WAC program on campus. Figure 7.1 illustrates a taxonomy of motivations as reported by faculty in response to the following survey question: *What are your motivations for having students write in [a chosen] course?* As the question was open-ended, some faculty provided more than one response, making the total of responses greater than the number of participants.

As depicted in Figure 7.1, the 381 total responses received from 220 faculty have been categorized into 12 types of motivations, with the greatest number of faculty (a little more than half) identifying *promote transferable skills* as a reason for emphasizing writing in an undergraduate course. While only two faculty actually used the term *transfer*, respondents indicated in very clear terms the importance they see in helping students develop transferable skills, whether in preparation for graduate school, their future professions, and/or life outside the classroom more generally. As one faculty wrote about students wishing to attend graduate school in the future,

> In Honors Courses, the goal is to promote student's engagement and experience with evidence-based practice and research. The majority of students in the course desire to obtain a graduate degree (MSN, DNP, or Ph.D.) in nursing, which requires writing skills. My goal in assigning written assignments is to promote their growth and development throughout our undergraduate program to ensure

advancement in their career trajectory.

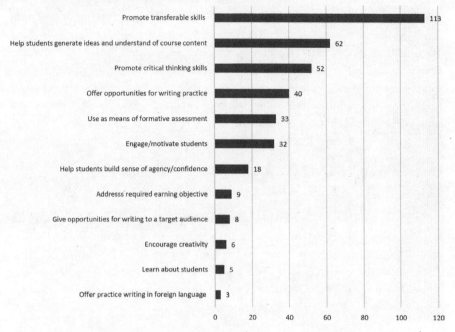

Figure 7.1. Faculty motivations for fostering undergraduate writing.

Another respondent, from the School of Architecture and Planning, wrote about students' development of their writing skills as a kind of duty of citizenry or community:

> I know the value of language (in general, and as [a] written record/communication) . . . I am motivated by the awareness of just how much the mis-use of language is responsible for bureaucratic insensitivity to reality, for political tribalism and fractured communities, and for interpersonal confusion, resentments, and even outright hatreds. Learning to write is a big step towards being able to contribute to solutions.

Faculty also recognized the generative aspect of writing as a tool for learning: "I am motivated for students to write-to-learn: to connect with their own thinking process and idea generation. This can serve as a foundation for communicating with each other about and exchanging their ideas about the subject matter"—as well as a tool for fostering critical thinking: "To teach brainstorming, critical thinking and reflection of course concepts. I want students to realize that the business concepts we teach are not purely objective; journaling, application, and reflection are also very important."

Additionally, a number of faculty identified students' need for practice as a motivation for assigning writing and as a means of formative or alternative assessment and a way to engage students in course work. Finally, additional reasons for assigning writing included fostering student confidence and agency in themselves as writers, teaching them to write for specific and varied audiences, encouraging creativity, faculty learning more about students, and practicing writing in a foreign language (i.e., other than their native language of English). To a much smaller degree, faculty identified writing as a required learning objective of the course, while other faculty commented that they included writing despite it not being listed as a required program or course outcome.

As reflected in the responses presented above, "[u]sing IE to study the 'work' that people carry out allows writing studies researchers to reveal the deep and often hidden investments and experiences of those people, making visible the values, practices, beliefs, and belongings that circulate below more visible or dominant discourses" while uncovering "opportunities for recognition, conversation, or intervention" (LaFrance 5). Clearly, the motivations that faculty have identified for supporting students' development as writers across the disciplines are well in line with the overall beliefs extolled by the field of writing studies as to how WAC work can serve students as developing writers. These include supporting students' transfer of knowledge and practice in writing across genres and contexts (Anson and Moore; Nowacek; Yancey et al.), understanding writing as generative (Preston; Thelin and Taczak), supporting students' development of critical thinking skills (Bean and Melzer; Brookfield; Carpenter and Krest; Carrithers et al.; Nosich), and using writing for formative or alternative assessments and to scaffold learning (Anderson, et al.; Childers; Gibbs and Simpson; Maki; Wiggins and McTighe).

With the identification of these faculty beliefs, as a WAC director I am able to reinforce the ways faculty value the use of undergraduate writing in their curriculum while also offering various kinds of support (e.g., effective means of using formative assessment, engaging students, and offering opportunities for writing to diverse audiences, etc.). The faculty responses above are indeed heartening, even ideal. However, as we know, faculty (would need to) enact such beliefs within an institutional context that often shapes faculty practices despite one's beliefs. As LaFrance reminds us, the work of an individual "is always rule-governed and textually mediated" by hierarchical forces within one's institutional context and often against one's own interests (5). As such, I was intrigued to learn from faculty what about their work with undergraduate writing, despite their motivations, made the work challenging and what might possibly negatively influence their commitment to WAC.

REVEALING TENSIONS AND CONTRADICTIONS WITH IE

As Rankin reminds us, the goal of IE research "is to investigate how people working in a particular place are coordinated by work going on elsewhere [within the institution] . . . [and] to amass evidence that is used to describe and to empirically explicate how disparate interests are activated and subordinated" ("Conducting" 2). The IE framework names this conflict of interests a *problematic*. LaFrance distinguishes problematic from a problem as such: While the former may begin with the latter, a problematic "then recognizes and accounts for the situated, complex, and interconnected relations among people, their experiences, and their practices related to that problem" (39). Annica Cox, in this collection, describes the revealing of problematics as a way to "explore further the persistent conflicts, slippages, and disjunctions in the work that we do, *despite* our best efforts." And, as LaFrance and Nicolas explain, "a problematic takes into account that not all individuals will be oriented to a situation or practice in the same way" (139). A problematic I have identified at UNM via this study is represented by the disjuncture between the seemingly widespread practice of integrating writing into courses across the disciplines and how that occurrence differs from what is "worked up (abstracted) within the official texts, policies, and understandings" (i.e., via the IE heuristic of boss texts)[6] of the larger institutional context (Rankin "Conducting . . . Analytical" 3).

While the majority of faculty respondents included 300- and 400-level courses in their disciplines as locations where they focus on undergraduate writing, writing instruction as official institutional policy at UNM is limited to a few first and second year "communication" courses as part of UNM's general education requirements ("Communication"). These courses are described by the institution as "complementing the major" and as "providing a base of knowledge and flexible tools for thinking" that "equip students for success throughout their education and after graduation" ("General Education Curriculum"). However, formal institution-wide policy in support of student writing stops there. The problematic or disjuncture, then, is between faculty's clear interest in and active participation with writing across the curriculum at higher levels of instruction in the disciplines (the "ideal") while not being offered formal support from the institution in doing this work, neither through stated policy nor, least of all, a well-established, well-funded WAC program (the "real"). Perhaps ironically,

---

6   See Nugent, et al. and other chapters in this collection for a detailed discussion of boss texts.

then, where others in this collection point to the tensions to be negotiated between "boss texts" and the embodied experiences of faculty work, this study points to the tension created by *a lack* of boss texts beyond first-year writing as evidence of the administration's disinterest in or failure to support faculty and students in undergraduate writing across the curriculum.

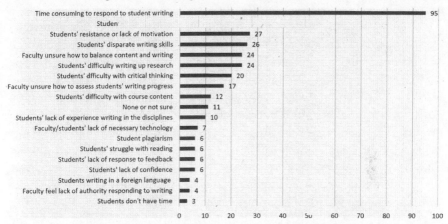

Figure 7.2. Faculty perceptions of barriers to assigning student writing in a course.

When comparing faculty motivations for supporting undergraduate student writing in their courses to the challenges faculty face with the practicalities of that work, additional problematics are revealed, specifically in response to the second of my survey questions: *What are challenges or barriers to having students write in [a chosen] course?* Figure 7.2 taxonomizes the 342 responses received from 216 faculty participants to that open-ended question, with some faculty providing more than one response.

While the *motivations* identified by faculty reveal the *theoretical* reasons why individuals might work to integrate writing into their undergraduate courses, the *challenges* identified by faculty point to the *material* conditions that can make the work of emphasizing writing in courses across the disciplines difficult. To some readers, it may appear at first glance that the responses in Figure 7.2 might be grouped into two categories: student and faculty "deficiencies." However, returning to Rankin's notion of standpoint as an IE heuristic, "The work of the IE analyst is to conduct inquiries into ruling practices from the standpoint of actual people who occupy specific locations within the extended ruling regimes that coordinate everyday work" ("Conducting" 2). This means we must consider the faculty standpoint expressed above within the material realities of the larger institutional context. We must consider the materiality of the university in which faculty are teaching and students are learning to understand more clearly the meaning of the responses above. As articulated by LaFrance, "IE as methodology poses the ongoing critical work of ethnography as a simultaneous process of theorizing our work within institutional contexts and as a means to understand the actualities of that work that live below the layers of our materialist discourse" (23). Faculty's responses to the second survey question help to uncover the reality that lies below the surface.

The most obvious challenge identified by 95 faculty (44%) as inhibiting their work is the amount of time (or lack thereof) that faculty have to respond to student writing. This challenge was identified almost three times more than the next challenge. Specifically, faculty described the time it takes to grade papers or provide useful feedback to students as "daunting" or "prohibitive" due to the institutional constraints of high student enrollment in a class, a high teaching load, and/or a lack of support from a course TA. Faculty also reported teaching classes ranging in size from 20 to 200 students and teaching up to 300 students per semester. Of course, the higher the enrollment for a class and the higher the teaching load, the less time a faculty member has to offer feedback to any one student. And within several of the disciplines on campus, it is often non-tenure track faculty who teach the undergraduate courses while carrying a higher teaching load, making responding to student writing almost, or often, impossible. Obviously, it is not faculty who set course caps or define teaching loads but department chairs, deans, or provosts. Such policies, then, have a negative effect on faculty's ability to support students in their development as writers.[7] This condition reflects the IE concept of *ruling relations*, which, as explained in the introduction to this collection, "shape thinking and doing within institutional settings, routines, and conditions [that] are not accidental, but bear traces of ideology, history, and social influence." The influence here at UNM are the austerity measures set by university administrators to make any one class mor profitable, despite the conflict it creates for best practices in teaching and support of student learning.

The additional challenges listed in Figure 7.2 might be viewed at first glance as owing to faculty or student shortcomings, as faculty have identified them. However, the additional challenges, upon closer examination, are also the result of ruling relations. For example, 24 faculty (11%) identify having difficulty balancing time and attention to writing instruction in class with that of the course content required by factors beyond their control: requirements identified by their department or program, the New Mexico Higher Education Department,

---

7   At my own institution, thankfully, the fire marshal has forced the administration, in a sense, to limit course caps for first-year writing (FYW) to 25 students, as the rooms available to the FYW program can accommodate only up to 25 students safely and legally. However, note that even this level of enrollment conflicts with the CCCC recommendation that writing classes be limited to no more than 20 students, with the ideal limit set at 15 (CCCC).

and other accrediting bodies, and/or the expectations of colleagues teaching more advanced content higher up the curriculum. Therefore, despite faculty valuing attention to undergraduate writing, the outcomes identified by the *ruling relations* coordinating and organizing the daily experiences and practices of faculty (and students) across space and time (LaFrance 32) make the focus on writing difficult, particularly without formal institutional support (in the way of a WAC program or other) on how to address these challenges.

The lack of access to faculty development opportunities in relation to WAC is also evident in other difficulties identified by faculty, including not being able to clearly communicate to students faculty expectations for an assignment (and "without being too prescriptive"), designing fair assessments, and successfully tracking students' progress with writing. A small number of faculty also identified (incorrectly, in my view) their lack of authority to offer students feedback on their writing, either because faculty themselves are non-native speakers of English (e.g., "I learned English starting at an adult age, and thus my English skills are limited, so I do not feel that I have full authority to teach how to write") or because they simply weren't sure how to respond to student writing effectively:

> We have students practice paraphrasing passages so they get more comfortable with that skill for larger stakes Wikipedia page edits. My challenge is that true paraphrasing is subjective and sometimes I don't feel confident in how I assess their paraphrases. Beyond advising that they don't reuse phrases from the original sentence, sometimes I lack the precision needed to communicate what they need to do to make their paraphrases better.

With IE's focus on the ruling relations that coordinate faculty's daily work, we can re-see the deficiencies that faculty view as their own as actually a failure of the institution to provide adequate support for faculty who value opportunities for undergraduate writing across the disciplines.

The failure of institutions, both at the university and state levels, is also reflected in what may first appear to some as student deficiencies. In Figure 7.2, faculty identified thirteen of nineteen challenges of writing instruction as those brought to the classroom by students. However, again, as IE instructs us, a closer examination, or a "looking up" as described by the editors and authors of this collection, reveals that the deficiencies ascribed to students are more accurately viewed as those of our local and state institutions that govern the experiences of faculty and students. For example, the particular challenges faculty identified as originating with students' orbit around differences in student's preparation before attending university and their subsequent disparate writing skills, including grammar knowledge, critical thinking skills, the ability to write up research, comprehension of course content, degree of experience writing in the disciplines, reading ability, and, to a lesser degree, understanding and avoiding plagiarism. At its most extreme, but, fortunately, to the least degree in response to the survey, blame placed on students appears in the form of classism and racism, as illustrated in the following faculty survey response that overgeneralizes the (lack of) ability among students from New Mexico in contrast with students from other states and other countries:

> Students come in from high school with woefully inadequate
> basic writing skills, and almost no research, synthesis, and
> factual interpretation skills whatsoever. This of course varies
> widely—a second challenge for a teacher. There are differences
> in preparedness between NM [New Mexico] and out of state
> students. In addition, [our] classes [in my discipline] attract a
> high proportion of foreign students, whose English ranges from
> superb (better than "native" speakers, actually) to abysmal.

As reflected here, we see that some faculty are conditioned to identify students and their writing as lacking[8][9] rather than recognizing the socially organized ruling practices at the institutional and state levels constructed by contemporary Western societies that result in differences in preparation among UNM students (Rankin "Conducting . . . Guidance" 2). Here, I return to the data from the Annie E. Casey Foundation referenced above that perhaps accounts for this faculty's perception of the variation of student preparedness. We know that in 2019 New Mexico was ranked at or near the bottom among the 50 states according to six indicators, including education (50th) and economics (49th) (9). We also know that an overwhelming majority of undergraduate students from New Mexico are both first generation college students and represent historically marginalized races/ethnicities. However, rather than label the institutional factors at the state and national levels that "have failed to eliminate the racial and ethnic inequalities" that contribute greatly to the variation in student preparedness within our state and local institutions, including K-12 public schools and colleges and universities, the deficiency at the institutional level is occluded and, too often, as here, placed on the student.[10]

---

8   See, for example, reference to UNM's past "remedial" English program via the UNM Newsroom before it was replaced by Stretch and Studio courses (Suilmann).

9   See Bethany Davila and Cristyn Elder's curriculum response to this issue.

10   Not to mention the problematic ideologies around language and standardization that are perpetuated by the institution and, therefore, at times, faculty. Again, see Davila and Elder's curriculum response to this issue.

At the same time, some faculty blame their own self-identified "deficiencies" for not knowing how to respond or not having the time to respond in an effective way to the perceived needs of students. In this way, attention to the university and the state's deficient response—through the withholding of human, monetary, or technical resources, to name a few, and the (lack of) implementation of (un)helpful policies—is displaced onto students and faculty, who are, in fact, subject to the ruling relations of the university and the state. With IE's emphasis on identifying the interconnections between the material conditions of the sites in which we work and how or why people do what they do, we begin to recognize how our practices are coordinated by institutional factors that often work against faculty and what we know as best practices for increased student success. With this tension brought out in the open with IE, we can in fact see the challenges identified by faculty in Figure 7.2 as material conditions of the university. We understand the needs of faculty and students. And we can see the ways our local and state institutions fail to address them.

CONCLUSION

We know from the collection of WAC scholarship over the years that three conditions are necessary for a WAC program to survive: 1) "grassroots and faculty support"; 2) "strong philosophical and fiscal support from institutional administrators"; and 3) a combination of one and two (Townsend 50–51). The overarching goal of this research has been to identify factors that may point to the first—a faculty commitment (or lack thereof) to WAC at UNM and where commitment may lie on campus so that it may be leveraged for broader, sustainable support for UNM's nascent WAC program. At the start of this research, I expected the data collected to help me "make visible [the] assumptions that underlie practices, anticipate points of resistance, determine which existing ideologies might be candidates for change, identify ideologies that clash, and plan strategies for handling those differences" as a step in measuring the possible commitment of faculty to sustainable WAC (Cox et al. 66). I have sought to identify some of the ideologies held by faculty, as well as the material conditions of their work, that can influence their teaching of undergraduate writing. Upon analyzing faculty responses to the two survey questions above—regarding faculty motivations and challenges to teaching writing—through the lens of IE "we can begin to see how notions of writing and its institutional contexts are co-created in the 'inter-individual' interplay among discursive structures, material actualities, and the work individuals carry out (Smith 2005)" (qtd. in LaFrance 28). This interplay of individual and institutional factors, or "discursive pivot points" as Devault refers to them (LaFrance 28), may either help or hinder (or both) a commitment to WAC as one's institutional context shapes conceptions of writing, including our own and of those around us, for good and for bad. The interest shown by faculty above in undergraduate writing, as evidenced by the response rate, across a wide range of undergraduate programs, surely points to a kind of interactivity that can be strengthened and built upon in a purposeful way toward sustainable WAC. Even more importantly, of course, in support of sustainable WAC are the ideologies underlying faculty's motivations for assigning undergraduate writing, which reflect the underlying beliefs of the field of writing studies about the ways WAC can serve students effectively. The support from faculty for WAC and across the disciplines is clearly represented in the data.

However, the material conditions faculty identify, co-constructed by the ruling relations of the institution, point to a lack of commitment from those who set the conditions for faculty teaching and student learning. Again, I evoke LaFrance: "As writing studies researchers begin to account for the complex interconnections between the material conditions of our sites and how people do what they do, we begin to recognize how writing, writing pedagogy, and our multifaceted work in sites of writing are coordinated by particular institutional factors" (5–6). IE, as my method of design and analysis for this study, has served to uncover the tensions and conflicts influencing faculty (and students') everyday practices against their own best interests, with high course enrollments, an emphasis on quantity rather than quality of course content, and an adherence to ineffective approaches to teaching and learning as reinforced by institutional austerity measures, not to mention the intersectional racist/classist systems reinforced by local and state institutions. While this initial research points to the clear presence of grassroots faculty support for WAC across schools, colleges, and disciplines on our Albuquerque campus, a question still remains: Will there be adequate support at the level of local and state institutions for sustainable WAC at UNM?

WORKS CITED

"2019 Kids Count Data Book: State Trends in Child Well-Being." *The Annie E. Casey Foundation*, https://www.aecf.org/resources/2019-kids-count-data-book. Accessed 15 Nov. 2022.

Anderson, Paul, et al. "How to Create High-Impact Writing Assignments that Enhance Learning and Development and Reinvigorate WAC/WID Programs: What Almost 72,000 Undergraduates Taught Us," *Across the Disciplines,* special issue: *WAC and High-Impact Practices,* edited by Beth Boquet and Neal Lerner, vol. 13, no. 4, 2016, https://doi.org/10.37514/ATD-J.2016.13.4.13.

Anson, Chris M., and Jessie L. Moore, editors. *Critical Transitions: Writing and the Question of Transfer.* The WAC Clearinghouse / UP of Colorado, 2016, https://doi.org/10.37514/PER-B.2016.0797.2.10.

Bean, John C., and Dan Melzer. *Engaging Ideas: The Professor's Guide to Integrative Writing, Critical Thinking, and Active Learning in the Classroom.* 3rd ed., Jossey-Bass, 2021.

Brookfield, Stephen D. *Teaching for Critical Thinking: Tools and Techniques to Help Students Question Their Assumptions.* Jossey-Bass, 2012.

Carpenter, J. Harrison, and Margie Krest. "It's about the Science: Students Writing and Thinking about Data in a Scientific Writing Course." *Language and Learning Across the Disciplines,* vol. 5 no. 2, 2001, pp. 1–20, https://doi.org/10.37514/LLD-J.2001.5.2.04.

Carrithers, David, et al. "Messy Problems and Lay Audiences: Teaching Critical Thinking within the Finance Curriculum." *Business Communication Quarterly,* vol. 71, no. 2, 2008, pp. 152–70, https://doi.org/10.1177/1080569908318202.

CCCC (2015). "CCCC Position Statement: Principles for the Postsecondary Teaching of Writing,*"* 2015, https://cccc.ncte.org/cccc/resources/positions/postsecondary writing#principle11

Childers, Pamela B. "Alternative Assessment Methods Across the Disciplines." *Alternatives to Grading Student Writing,* edited by Stephen Tchudi, NCTE [ERIC Document Reproduction Service, ED 409 577], 1997, pp. 296–300.

"Communication." *General Education.* University of New Mexico. https://gened.unm.edu/areas-of-study/index.html. Accessed 27 Nov. 2022.

Cox, Michelle, et al. *Sustainable WAC: Launching and Developing Writing Across the Curriculum Programs.* NCTE, 2018.

Davila, Bethany A., and Cristyn L. Elder. "Welcoming Linguistic Diversity and Saying Adiós to Remediation: Stretch and Studio Composition at a Hispanic-Serving Institution." *Composition Forum,* vol. 35, 2017, http://compositionforum.com/issue/35/new-mexico.php.

"Fall 2019 Official Enrollment Report Albuquerque Campus." University of New Mexico, 6 Sept. 2019. http://oia.unm.edu/facts-and-figures/documents/Enrollment%20Reports/fall-2019-oer.pdf.

"First Gen Proud." University of New Mexico. https://firstgen.unm.edu/. Accessed 17 Nov. 2022.

"General Education Curriculum." General Education. University of New Mexico. https://gened.unm.edu/index.html. Accessed 17 Nov. 2022.

Gibbs, Graham, and Claire Simpson. "Conditions Under Which Assessment Supports Student Learning." *Learning and Teaching in Higher Education,* vol. 1, 2004, pp. 3–31. https://www.researchgate.net/publication/237063306_Conditions_Under_Which_Assessment_Supports_Students'_Learning.

LaFrance, Michelle. *Institutional Ethnography: A Theory of Practice for Writing Studies Researchers.* Utah State UP, 2019.

LaFrance, Michelle and Melissa Nicolas. "Institutional Ethnography as Materialist Framework for Writing Program Research and the Faculty-Staff Work Standpoints Project." *CCC,* vol. 64, no. 1, 2012, pp. 130–50.

Maki, Peggy L. "Developing an Assessment Plan to Learn about Student Learning." *The Journal of Academic Librarianship*, vol. 28, no. 1, 2002, pp. 8–13.

Nosich, Gerald M. *Learning to Think Things Through: A Guide to Critical Thinking Across the Curriculum*. 3rd ed., Pearson Education, 2009.

Nowacek, Rebecca. *Agents of Integration: Understanding Transfer as a Rhetorical Act.* NCTE, 2011.

Preston, Jacqueline. "Project(ing) Literacy: Writing to Assemble in a Postcomposition FYW Classroom." *College Composition and Communication*, vol. 67, no. 1, 2015, pp. 35–63.

Rankin, Janet. "Conducting Analysis in Institutional Ethnography: Analytical Work Prior to Commencing Data Collection." *International Journal of Qualitative Methods,* vol. 16, 2017, pp. 1–9. https://doi.org/10.1177/1609406917734484.

———. "Conducting Analysis in Institutional Ethnography: Guidance and Cautions." *International Journal of Qualitative Methods,* vol. 16, 2017, pp. 1–11. https://doi.org/10.1177/1609406917734472.

Suilmann, Joe. "UNM discontinues remedial Introductory Studies courses." *UNM Newsroom*, 27 Oct. 2015, http://news.unm.edu/news/unm-discontinues-remedial-introductory-studies-courses.

Thelin, William H., and Kara Taczak. "Generative Themes and At-Risk Students." *Teaching English in the Two-Year College,* vol. 34, no. 3, 20007, pp. 295–305.

Townsend, Martha. "WAC Program Vulnerability and What to Do About It: An Update and Brief Bibliographic Essay." *The WAC Journal*, vol. 19, 2008, pp. 45–61. https://doi.org/10.37514/WAC-J.2008.19.1.04.

Wiggins, Grant, and Jay McTighe. *Understanding By Design*, 2nd ed., Assn. for Supervision & Curriculum Development, 2005.

Yancey, Kathleen Blake, et al. *Writing Across Contexts: Transfer, Composition, and Sites of Writing*. Utah State UP, 2014.

CHAPTER 8.

IE AND PEDAGOGICAL POSSIBILITIES: A FRAMEWORK FOR THIRDSPACE EXPLORATIONS

Michelle Miley with Anna Couch, Juliana Greene, Hannah Telling, and Lauren Adams Turner

Montana State University

> At least temporarily, set aside the demands to make an either/ or choice and contemplate instead the possibility of a both/and also logic. . . . [Thirdspace] is . . . an efficient invitation to enter a space of extraordinary openness, a place of critical exchange where the geographical imagination can be expanded to encompass a multiplicity of perspectives that have heretofore been considered by the epistemological referees to be incompatible, uncombinable.
>
> —Edward Soja, *Thirdspace: Journeys to Los Angeles and Other Real-and-Imagined-Places*

My impulse to start in practice and to work towards theory is perhaps what drew me to Edward Soja's Thirdspace theory. I discovered Soja while incorporating Rhonda Grego and Nancy Thompson's studio model into our writing in the disciplines program at a previous institution. My simple understanding of Soja's theory is this: First space, representing the ideal or what we believe "should be," rarely is a mirror image of second space, representing "reality," or "what is." The space between first and second—thirdspace—reveals the lived, material space where those two collide. When we pay attention to thirdspace, we can begin to understand how our lived spaces form, and we can begin to bring the "ideal" and the "real" into better alignment. As I've written elsewhere, Soja, whose explanation of thirdspace as a collision between the ideal and the real, helped me articulate the gaps between what I was learning in my study of rhetoric and writing studies and what I saw in the students' lived experiences of writing when they came into the writing center ("Writing Studio").

The world we are living in at this moment in time has me reflecting often on thirdspace. We have become a society fixed in an either/or logic, desperately in need of the flexible space for critical exchange, for both/and also thinking, that thirdspace offers. Those who are in college now and who will be entering our

DOI: https://doi.org/10.37514/PER-B.2023.2029.2.08

classrooms in the foreseeable future have come of age during this time of deep polarization. The public world they live in has given them access to either/or thinking but has not often modeled the complexity and nuance of both/and also thinking. And stepping into thirdspace does not come naturally; these are not comfortable spaces. Stepping into that gap between ideal and real, Soja warns, "can provide daunting challenges to practical understanding and application" (22). Acknowledging when our ideals do not match up to material experiences can leave us feeling unmoored, anxious, in despair, frightened. I would argue, however, that exploring thirdspace becomes more and more necessary to our survival as our world becomes more divided.

But to explore thirdspace, Soja argues, "requires a strategic and flexible way of thinking that is guided by a particular motivating project, a set of clear practical objectives and preferred pathways that will help to keep each individual journey on track while still allowing for lateral excursions to other spaces, times, and social situations" (22). We need structured frameworks, methodologies, to keep us on our path. Institutional ethnography, with its focus on beginning in the lived, material experience of those doing the work and then looking up to map the web of relationships, has become one such way of strategic thinking for me, helping me navigate through the collisions between what I imagine to be ideal and what happens in the real. Through IE, the complex, relational activity of my own work and the work of others becomes visible. When IE guides my thinking, I am able to explore the thirdspaces I encounter.

Because I understand my teaching work to include showing others how language both connects and divides us, how it shapes our thinking, and thus how it shapes our world, I believe it is also my responsibility now more than ever to also offer strategies for navigating the thirdspace complexities such study requires. Others have offered ethnographic frameworks as such a process of inquiry for under-graduate students, noting that ethnographic processes offer students the ability to see writing as social, to connect with community, and to conduct critical inquiry (Malley and Hawkins). I, too, have seen how ethnography can positively shape the experiences we create for our students. And I have also seen how IE offers students a visibility of the interrelatedness and interdependence of individuals and institutions. With its insistence of starting in standpoint and mapping up to ruling relations, IE offers a view of how, as LaFrance notes in Chapter One, "practice emerges in a unique relationship to the values and relationships that situate, compel and organize both ephemeral and more stable patterns of activity. . . . [how l] ocal discourse compels (but does not determine) the shape of our practice" (28).

The visibility of the interrelatedness of discourse and practice, of individuals and institutions, is a valuable one not just for researchers but also for our students. I would like to add to our pedagogical frameworks institutional ethnography, using as an example an institutional ethnography I conducted in 2018–2019 with a team of four undergraduate tutor researchers. Although the chapter will draw from the research project as an example of IE as a framework for thirdspace exploration, I will focus primarily on the experience of the undergraduate tutor researchers rather than on the findings from the study.

The voices of the undergraduate tutors—Anna Couch, Juliana Greene, Hannah Telling, and Lauren Adams Turner—will come through their 2019 IWCA conference presentations, our conversations both before and after our inquiry, and our emails. What their stories show is the power of IE as a strategic way of exploring and beginning to understand not only the collision spaces between the ideals of institutions and the reality of lived experiences, but also how those ideals come into existence. With IE as our framework, together we began to explore how a group of students often considered "at-risk" in the "ideal" of the institution, understood the work of academic writing. We began to see how our pedagogical ideals were sometimes disrupted in the lived reality of those students. The undergraduate tutor researchers noted that with its insistence on starting with the material experience of those who do the work and then mapping it to understand how things happen within institutions, IE provided a framework that was useful for making concrete, in ways other experiences had not, how we act and are acted upon in the world. IE became for all of us a tool for thirdspace exploration, and, for me, a pedagogical framework I had been looking for. I offer our experience together as a reflection on and example of how IE can be useful as a methodology for students learning to navigate the complexities of both/and also thinking.

STANDPOINT – WHO DOES THE MATERIAL WORK OF ACADEMIC WRITING?

The research project the tutor researchers and I conducted emerged from a discussion at the 2016 International Writing Centers Association annual conference. At the conference, I attended a reader's workshop of Leigh Patel's *Decolonizing Educational Research* during which we brainstormed how we might design our research studies to honor our students' cultures and educational desires. One participant who had read my earlier work suggested to me that IE, grounded in the experience of those doing the work, provides a way to begin from the students' experiences. Since students are the population materially "doing" the work of academic writing, and are the population writing centers should be supporting, these student voices are imperative for us to hear.[1] With an internal grant from my

---

1   Until this discussion, I had grounded my IE research on the work of writing centers from the knowledge and experience of the administrator (Miley "Mapping," "Looking").

institution, followed by an IWCA research grant, I set out to develop just such a study beginning with the standpoint of the students. I first began the research of mapping student perceptions of academic writing in the fall of 2017. I designed the project so that the undergraduate research tutors would interview students, following Michelle Eodice, Anne Geller, and Neal Lerner's model. In the first year of the study, the tutors and I recruited widely. Because the research team happens to be made up of one engineering and one science major, we discovered our interviews were skewed to engineering students in their senior year. We realized that while interesting, what those students understood the work of academic writing to be might not represent the population of students we most needed to hear from. Because the writing center had been partnering with a new program at our institution designed to offer support to students often considered "at-risk" for economic, social, or academic reasons, and because we knew we would like to better understand those students' needs, in the second year of our study, the team of researchers made up of Juliana, Hannah, Lauren, Anna, and I focused on the Hilleman Scholars program. That is the year from which this chapter draws.

The Hilleman Scholars, instituted in 2016, named after Dr. Maurice Hilleman, is a program providing "worthy high school graduates from Montana with exceptional financial and academic support throughout their four years at MSU so that they, too, can realize their full potential and actively contribute to their communities" (Hilleman Scholars Program). In its ideal, the Hilleman Scholars program provides financial and academic support for a population of students that typically struggles to navigate higher education. During the first years of the program, scholars enrolled in a summer math and writing class (WRIT 100) designed to prepare them for first semester writing (WRIT 101). The writing center provides support for the Scholars on their writing during the Summer Success Academy.[2] Hannah, Lauren, Juliana, and Anna were tutors in the summer program. From the beginning, we noticed gaps between our understanding of the work of the summer writing class, the writing instructors' understanding, the program's understanding, and the scholars. Our IE formed out of our need to explore this gap: we wondered, how did the Scholars understand the work of academic writing that they were being asked to do?[3]

---

2   In 2019, the program discontinued the writing class and designed a freshman seminar class. They cited a desire for students to receive credit towards graduation, which they did not receive taking WRIT 100. However, because the freshman seminar class is writing intensive, and because the administrators of the program wanted the scholars to connect with the writing center, we continue to work with Hilleman Scholars each summer.

3   Although we came to our problematic because we saw the gaps between the ideals of the summer writing course curriculum and the students' lived experience of the class, we chose to work specifically from the standpoint of the students so that we could better understand what they understood as the work of academic writing.

In the first semester of our study, Juliana, Hannah, and Lauren recruited 16 interviewees from the Hilleman Scholars program. Anna joined the project later, offering her own experience as a first-generation college student writer through autoethnography,[4] bringing her lived experience to our IE mapping as a data point that allowed us to see how beyond the Hilleman program to the larger system of ruling relations in our educational institutions. Because "the IE framework shifts the ethnographer's eye away from reified or static understandings of the people, events, or sites studied," the methodology invited the students into a practice of embodiment, making visible how "individuals within a location co-create the dynamics and processes under investigation" (LaFrance 5). In the classroom, our students do not often experience research that begins in material, lived experiences. By starting our project grounded in the Hilleman Scholars' experiences and then mapping up, the tutor researchers made visible the collision spaces between our understanding of the ideals of academic writing and the material experiences of those enacting those ideals. Starting from the standpoint of the scholars, we began our thirdspace exploration.

I immediately noted how grounding our project in the material, lived experiences of the scholars, and using a number of heuristics for IE (Elder, this collection), allowed our team to map up and see the larger web of activity that created the understanding of what the work of writing is in the academy. Although the structures of a classroom experience and the limitations of a 15-week semester make a full institutional ethnography difficult, I have used standpoint and mapping up as a frame in later conversations with tutors as well as with the students I am teaching in the classroom to make webs of activity more visible for them. In the writing center, I often overhear students working through rhetorical concepts, able to define terms like "rhetorical context," "exigence," or even "audience" in the theoretical abstract but struggling to fully understand how they apply those concepts to the situations in which and about which they write.[5] When students learn IE as a methodology, when they learn to begin with the material, lived experience that starting in standpoint provides, they have a

---

4   In 2019, Lauren, Juliana, and I presented what we had learned from our study at the International Writing Centers Association/ National Conference on Peer Tutoring in Writing Conference in Columbus, Ohio. Because Hannah was also presenting at the conference, we were able to continue to keep her in our conversations. Lauren focused her presentation on explaining institutional ethnography as a methodology, and Juliana provided findings from her analysis of the interviews. Anna expanded our analysis through her autoethnography.

5   In her recent longitudinal study, Anne Ruggles Gere found that undergraduate students particularly had difficulty understanding audience. "In interviews, a number of students said they would 'just write' with no thought about the reader. The need to consider imagined or actual audiences, including what that audience knows and needs to know and their reasons for reading a given text, were largely beyond their ken" (21).

concrete strategy for thinking through the gaps between what is often a very abstract ideal and the lived experiences of our complex webs of relations. As our study continued, we found, similarly to Erin Workman, Madeline Crozier, and Peter Vandenburg (this collection), that IE "continued to reshape our understanding of the problematics we set out to explore."

DISRUPTING ACADEMIC IDEALS: FROM PROBLEM TO PROBLEMATIC

IE made visible one thirdspace moment almost immediately. As the tutor researchers and I designed our study, we realized how important—and possibly how countercultural—IE's focus on "problematic" rather than "problem" was. Our team quickly discovered that shifting to problematic thinking pushes against what we have learned as the academic ideal. As actors in an educational institution that values and prioritizes scientific research methods, the undergraduate tutors came to our project understanding research as an objective, solution-oriented activity. The shift to "problematic" as a viable research focus did not come naturally. It took some time and discussion for us to move to a mindset that we were not "solving" any problems we might discover within the Hilleman program but rather making visible the heretofore invisible web of coordinated relations that shaped the academic writing experience of the Hilleman students.

In her conference presentation, Lauren described how shifting from "problem" to "problematic" changes the perspective of a researcher. "When we see something as a problem," she explained, we have a tendency to look for the cause of the problem, to place blame. We also tend to focus on a narrow view, fixated on how to "fix" the problem in front of us. "Problematics," Lauren explained, "encourage us to look at the greater context of the institution and examine which structures and patterns are giving rise to the problem we initially observed" (Adams Turner "Crafting"). Lauren then told about her experience reading an article on the Hilleman Scholars in the local newspaper, one that described the "Hilleman program as a 'remedial' program that helped 'save' students who, without the help of the program, would not be able to graduate college."[6] She noted that the article did not reflect her own perception or experience with the Hilleman program but that because the article was a text she viewed as authoritative, she began to question her own understanding of the Scholars program. In her words, she "began to see the work of the Hilleman program and even the Hilleman scholars as a 'problem'—something that needed to be fixed." What

---

6   We began to see the overlapping institutions—our institution of higher ed overlapping with the greater community's institutions. IE provides a methodology to see the relationships between these overlapping institutions, as Elisabeth Miller writes in this collection.

the framework of IE helped her to do was shift away from the "problem" that needed fixing to ask "how did this happen? "If the work of Hilleman scholars is being perceived as 'remedial,' what social or structural patterns might be in place at MSU that position their work that way? . . . [IE]'s idea of 'problematics' gives me the language and the eyes to begin questioning how the work of Hilleman scholars is institutionally organized and valued" (Adams Turner).

Any of us who perform qualitative research have had to push against the academic valuing of objective research. To put subjectivity, individual perceptions, back into our understanding requires us to resist what we have learned is "good research" from a young age. But what I hear from Lauren's narrative goes beyond valuing subjectivity as well as objectivity. What IE has offered her is a mindset that asks her to see a gap and ask, "how did this happen," to explore the full web of social relations. I hear in her explanation an understanding that "how things happen" is often complicated, a result of the web of forces that lead us neither to "right" or "wrong" ideal but rather to an awareness of "what is." As Juliana explained, with IE as a framework, we have to slow down long enough to understand how individuals' work coordinates within the contexts in which we live. She explained that we were using IE as "LaFrance and Nicolas wrote, 'to uncover *how things happen*—how institutional discourse compels and shapes practice(s) and how norms of practices speak to, for, and over individuals' (130). If we learn *how things happen* in the writing of the Hilleman Scholars, then we can learn *how things happen* in our writing center and tutoring sessions" (Greene "Crafting" her emphasis).

In a later email to the tutor researchers, I asked them what shifting from problem to problematic meant for them. Juliana responded, "When I think of IE as not coming up with a solution, I think of a solution as something being imposed on a situation without understanding of that situation, while IE as mapping provides a larger understanding of the context" (Greene email). She continued to explain the importance of working towards a goal of understanding rather than solving, referring to Krista Ratcliffe's (2005) explanation of understanding as "standing under discourses that surround us and others while consciously acknowledging all our particular—and very fluid—standpoints" (28). She noted, "I think that IE lets us do this through mapping because we are not given one answer or one situation to impose a solution on, (sic) we are given multiple experiences, actors, and situations where there can never be one solution, only an understanding of the larger context that created what we are attempting to understand" (Greene email). By shifting to problematic, the tutor-researchers began exploring from a both/and logic rather than the either/or logic of a problem mindset. They saw the Scholars *and themselves* as actors within a "complex, dynamic, flexible, multifaceted, layered, and shapeshifting site," one in which many of their practices would continue to be "scripted for [them] but that [each Scholar] will also actively negotiate these points of institutional contact in highly personal and unique ways" (LaFrance 39).

Our world is one that values quick solutions to problems. Our educational system reflects those values. Solutions are often easy to imagine in an either/or world. Learning to navigate both/and also logic, however, requires us to understand how something came into existence rather than simply focusing on how to fix it. In an educational system where students understand their work as an academic researcher/writer to be that of "solving a problem," of "fixing" a situation so that it is "what should be" rather than "what is," an IE way of thinking moves us away from "problem-thinking" to "problematic-thinking," offering students a tool to recognize the gaps between what they understood as "should be" with "what is" and "how it came to be." Such thinking offers them a way of better navigating through and actively participating in the world around them.

MAPPING UP: STANDPOINT TO RULING RELATIONS

By beginning with the student's standpoint and focusing on the problematic, the tutors and I were better able to practice the embodiment necessary for making visible the web of coordinated relations that shapes the academic writing experience. As we began to "look up" from the individual standpoint of the Hilleman Scholars and map their narratives of the work of writing to the individuals and texts that mediated their understanding of that work, the tutor researchers and I explored how the Hilleman Scholars "negotiated the site of their work in alignment with the ruling relations, entrenched patterns of labor and expertise and other expectations and understandings of the site" (LaFrance 67).[7]

We knew from our experience with the program that tension existed between the ideal communicated within the summer preparatory writing course (WRIT 100) and the lived experiences of the Scholars. This tension, rather than empowering the Scholars, often left them unsure how to move forward with their writing. As we interviewed the students, we began to hear in their words the gaps between their perceptions of the work of academic writing and what they were hearing in their WRIT 100 class. In Juliana's analysis of the interview transcripts, she observed that the scholars perceived "the work of writing [expressed in WRIT 100] to be a tool to express their identity" (Greene "Crafting"). In one interview, for example, a student describes the first day in the WRIT 100 class.

---

7   We find LaFrance's explanation of ruling relations in the introduction to this collection to be useful. Particularly, our project helped us understand that "[r]uling relations carry ideas, language, and rhetorical frameworks between individuals (even those with little personal interaction), impose ideals of practice and affiliation."

She reports that her instructor told them that the instructor did not want to ever see "the five-paragraph format that they had you write in high school and middle school" again. Instead, the instructor communicated valuing hearing about the students' own identities, experiences, opinions—all in direct opposition to what they had been taught in high school. The student said it took about a quarter of the course "to kind of realize it's okay to have your own opinion and to talk about your own opinion in your writing . . . and so it's given more, voice, it's given more body to how I write." For this Hilleman Scholar who had learned the five-paragraph essay as the way writing "should be," to have a new ideal posited in the class that totally threw out what she had learned before created a thirdspace gap. Her lived experience as an academic writer had to reconcile what she had been given as "should be" in high school with the "should be" of WRIT 100. She was asked to give up her way of knowing when she entered the WRIT 100 classroom without a clear understanding of why.[8]

Although the ideals communicated by the WRIT 100 instructor was one the tutors and I knew well from our own scholarship in writing studies, we saw the gap between those ideals and the reality of what others in the academy understood as the work of academic writing. When we began to map Anna's autoethnography alongside the interviews, this gap became even more visible. Anna's experience of college writing began not with WRIT 100 but with WRIT 101, our university's freshman writing course. In her autoethnography, Anna articulated her understanding of academic writing as "a way to show what I knew from class lecture and as a way to show what I had learned from researching and making connections to the text" (Couch "Crafting"). Mapping up from Anna's experience and those of the scholars, Juliana and Anna analyzed the WRIT 100 and 101 course descriptions:

> The WRIT 101 description says that its learning outcome is
> to "Demonstrate ability to read rhetorical situations" ("Core
> 2.0"). The WRIT 100 description, on the other hand, says
> that "Ultimately, our hope is that students understand them-
> selves differently as writers, setting them on the path to meet
> the writing challenges in their college classes and beyond"
> ("Hilleman Scholars"). Instead of being taught to think of
> one's self rhetorically, which is often a process of familiariz-
> ing yourself with the different ways you can write and have

---

8   Harry Denny, John Nordlof, and Lori Salem found a similar gap in the ideals professed by writing centers and the experiences of working-class students. They write, "For working-class students, writing centers evoke the feelings of dislocation and discomfort that come from mismatched implicit assumptions: we are not what they expect us to be, and we do not do what they expect us to do" (71).

written, WRIT 100 is asking the Hilleman scholars to think
differently about themselves, to defamiliarize themselves with
who they thought they were as writers. This lesson of defa-
miliarization is also something Denny and Towle resonate
with. They write that "To belong in an academic setting as
a first-generation student, one must give up what's familiar,
comfortable and known." (Denny and Towle 5)

Juliana noted that the gaps between their previous experiences of writing and
the ideals communicated by the WRIT 100 class often left the Hilleman Scholars paralyzed. "Most of the sessions went the same; we sat with a blank Google
doc in front of us and a worried expressions on both of our faces. How can you
start all over again from nothing?" (Greene "Crafting").

To help us continue mapping up, Lauren brought in texts describing the
work of the larger institution. Our institution is a land grant institution. Our
identity as such is important to the shaping of our institution; like Miller's "Wisconsin Idea" (this collection), the land grant mission serves as a "boss text" for
our university. Students have access to many documents describing our role as
a land grant institution, and Lauren had previously studied several histories of
land grant institutions for another class. Drawing from these texts, she connected the tension Hilleman Scholars might feel between the understanding
of work coming from the institution and that articulated in their WRIT 100
experience:

[A]s a Land Grant institution, MSU values writing because
it prepares students to get a good job. Understanding writing solely as "self-expression" prevents students from writing
rhetorically for different purposes and for different audiences,
as they would be required to in jobs. The ruling relation of
"writing as self-expression" and the ruling relation of the Land
Grant mission came in conflict with one another. (Adams
Turner)

Beginning from the standpoint of the Hilleman Scholars and mapping up to
the ruling relations represented in our work texts provided a better understanding of the thirdspace the Scholars were experiencing in WRIT 100. It also helped
us understand why the Hilleman Summer Success program decided in 2019 to
eliminate WRIT 100 as an experience and replace it with a career preparation
course. The gaps between the reality of the Hilleman program and the ideals
of the WRIT 100 curriculum design were too great. We confirmed LaFrance's
observation that "these materialities make a difference in how we do what we do;

we are also always negotiating local values, histories, hierarchies, and established work processes" (LaFrance 66). The maps made visible for us how the writing we engage in when in the academy are a "process of co-constitution" (66), ringing in the texts and mapping them to the experiences of the scholars, thinking through how those experiences came into being, made ruling relations—and the social and rhetorical nature of writing that exist within those ruling relations—visible.

CONCLUSION: IE AS THIRDSPACE EXPLORATION

As the tutor-researchers and I reflected on our experience of our research study, they articulated how IE became for them a framework through which they made visible the coordinated activity within their worlds. Like Dorothy Smith, we all noted paying attention to what before was the abstract activity that coordinated the experience of our work. Anna described that she began to understand "how language can both form community and [build] shared meaning of something . . . I'm really interested in applying IE to other aspects [of my life]" (Couch "Importance"). She observed that the experience with IE gave her the space and the time to "pause and reflect and think about" the ways in which we act and are acted upon in the world.

For all of the scholars, the maps IE provided gave them a sense of their own agency in their world, particularly as they thought through how to advocate for themselves and others. When I asked them how IE shifted/refined/honed their awareness or understanding of how "texts" coordinate work, Hannah, an English education major, noted, "[I]t made me think or understand . . . how texts in certain people's hands can become a mechanism for policing behavior. Both for the Hilleman project and then after the research project I noticed how people in my life or in my classes would use texts to almost police my behavior and get me to fit their idea of [how] a student in a discipline should act" (Telling "Discussion"). Hannah described, for example, the institutional texts in higher ed that mandated what teachers cover within any given course. She described the documents that she received as a student teacher that told her what she "should" do as a teacher.

Hannah was planning her graduation as we were wrapping up our discussions of our project. I asked her how her experience with IE would shape how she imagined her not-so-future work as an educator. She replied, "I definitely know I am going to want to be involved in the union at whatever job I end up in and be involved there—it's another discourse community with more texts—IE will be so helpful in navigating those worlds" (Telling "Discussion").

Anna was more hesitant, noting that, while she "definitely [could] see how the context affects the relationship," she was going to have to think about how change might occur. Reflecting, Anna said, "Are we ever in a context where the people in power are willing to change? . . . [Are] people in power willing to change?" (Couch personal interview).

Perhaps the first step to change is simply making visible/ mapping context. In Anna's final paper for her independent research study on our project together, she wrote:

> So, what now? How can writing studies include the rhetorical situation so students can write about the self and gain agency in the academic discourse? LeCourt writes, "If rhetorical situations attempt to 'stabilize' identity, then they also can potentially announce their identity work . . . students are not unaware of the identity work academic discourse may be seeking to perform. Such awareness represents an opportunity to intervene at the site of difference, with the moments at which difference is being produced" (47).

Anna's "what now" echoes in my thinking about how to bring institutional ethnography and its ability to, as Anna said at one point, "lift the veil" to reveal the complex webs in which we live to my pedagogical practices. My experience practicing institutional ethnography with Anna, Hannah, Juliana, and Lauren shows the possibilities for IE experiences in undergraduate education. Our experience enabled me to think about how to make concrete the social nature of writing for students. I discovered how to make visible thirdspace. From these experiences, we could better map how language and texts mediate our world. Anna, in her final essay "The Importance of Cultural Capital," says it well: "Institutional ethnography . . . can be used as a way of thinking that reminds us of the complex relationships not only in writing centers but within the institutions that writing centers are in. As the context is important in the rhetorical relationship, so is the context of an institution and the individuals within the institution" (qtd. in Le Court 47). In Lauren's words, "IE humanizes institutions," making visible the complex relationships of the work of living together. By providing IE as a strategic framework for thirdspace exploration, we do not simply offer our students a way to make the complex web of relations of writing more visible; rather, with its focus on experiential knowing through standpoint theory, its shift from finding solutions to mapping the terrain (a shift from problem to problematic), and its ability to make visible the web of ruling relations in which students enact their lives, I believe IE offers them as it does us a strategic way to see and explore thirdspace. It allows them to consider both/and rather than simply either/or. And in the worlds in which we live, both/and logic is a valuable—if not necessary—ability to have.

WORKS CITED

Adams Turner, Lauren. "Crafting Institutional Relationships." International Writing Centers Association/National Conference on Peer Tutoring in Writing Joint Conference, October 2019, Columbus, OH. Unpublished conference paper.

———. Personal interview with author. 13 Apr. 2020.

Couch, Anna. 2019. "Crafting Institutional Relationships." International Writing Centers Association/National Conference on Peer Tutoring in Writing Joint Conference, October 2019, Columbus, OH. Unpublished conference paper.

———. 2020. "The Importance of Cultural Capital: Navigating College Writing Expectations as a Frist-Generation Student." Final research paper submitted to author, Montana State U, *Independent Study, Fall 2019.*

———. Personal interview with author. 13 Apr. 2020.

Core 2.0. Montana State University. http://catalog.montana.edu/core-general -curricular-requirements/. Accessed 30 Aug. 2020.

Denny, Harry, and Beth Towle. "Braving the Waters of Class: Performance, Intersectionality, and the Policing of Working Class Identity." *The Peer Review,* vol. 1, no. 2, 2017. https://tinyurl.com/56sh76c8.

Denny, Harry, et al. "Tell me exactly what it was that I was doing that was so bad": Understanding the Needs and Expectations of Working-Class Students in Writing Centers." *Writing Center Journal,* vol. 37, no. 1, 2014, pp. 67–100.

Eodice, Michele, et al. *The Meaningful Writing Project: Learning, Teaching, and Writing in Higher Education.* Utah State UP, 2016.

Gere, Anne Ruggles, editor. *Developing Writers in Higher Education: A Longitudinal Study.* University of Michigan Press, 2019. https://doi.org/10.3998/mpub.1007 9890.

Greene, Juliana. "Crafting Institutional Relationships." International Writing Centers Association/National Conference on Peer Tutoring in Writing Joint Conference, October 2019, Columbus, OH. Unpublished conference paper.

———. "Re: Follow-up question about IE." Email to the author. 15 May 2020.

———. Personal interview with author. 13 Apr. 2020.

Grego, Rhonda C., and Nancy S. Thompson. *Teaching/Writing in Thirdspaces: The Studio Approach.* Southern Illinois UP, 2018.

Hilleman Scholars. Montana State University. https://www.montana.edu/hilleman scholars/. Accessed 30 Aug. 2020.

LaFrance, Michelle. *Institutional Ethnography: A Theory of Practice for Writing Studies Researchers.* Utah State UP, 2019.

LaFrance, Michelle, and Melissa Nicolas. "Institutional Ethnography as Materialist Framework for Writing Program Research and the Faculty-Staff Work Standpoints Project." *College Composition and Communication,* vol. 64, no. 1, 2012, pp. 130–50. https://www.jstor.org/stable/23264923.

LeCourt, Donna. "Performing Working-Class Identity in Composition: Toward a Pedagogy of Textual Practice." *College English,* vol. 69, no. 1., 2006, pp. 30–51. https://doi.org/10.2307/25472187.

Malley, Susan Blum, and Ames Hawkins. "Introduction." *Engaging Communities: Writing Ethnographic Research.* http://www.engagingcommunities.org/introduction/.

Miley, Michelle. "Looking Up and Out: Mapping Writing Center Work through Institutional Ethnography." *The Writing Center Journal,* vol. 36, no. 1, 2017, pp. 103–29. https://www.jstor.org/stable/44252639.

———. "Mapping Boundedness and Articulating Interdependence Between Writing Centers and Writing Programs." *Praxis: A Writing Center Journal,* vol. 16, no. 1, 2018, http://www.praxisuwc.com/161-miley.

———. "The Writing Studio as Countermonument: Reflexive Moments from Online Studios in Writing Center Partnerships." *The Writing Studio Sampler,* edited by Mark Sutton and Sally Chandler. The WAC Clearinghouse / UP of Colorado, 2018. pp. 167–83. https://doi.org/10.37514/PER-B.2018.0179.2.10.

Patel, Leigh. *Decolonizing Educational Research: From Ownership to Answerability.* Routledge, 2015.

Ratcliffe, Krista. *Rhetorical Listening: Identification, Gender, Whiteness.* Southern Illinois UP, 2005.

Smith, Dorothy. *Institutional Ethnography: A Sociology for People.* AltiMira Press, 2005.

Soja, Edward. *Thirdspace: Journeys to Los Angeles and Other Real-and-Imagined Places.* Blackwell, 1966.

Telling, Hannah. "Crafting Institutional Relationships." International Writing Centers Association/National Conference on Peer Tutoring in Writing Joint Conference, 16–19 Oct. 2019, Columbus, OH. Keynote address.

———. Personal interview with author. 13 Apr. 2020.

CONTRIBUTORS

Reema Barlaskar is a Special Lecturer in the Department of Writing and Rhetoric at Oakland University. Her doctoral research focuses on literacy, authorship, and women's writing and reading practices in the long nineteenth century. She teaches writing as a process grounded in reflection and community, focusing on digital rhetoric and literacy as foundational methods in academic discourse and research.

Ruth Book is Lecturer and Coordinator of the Writing Center in the University Writing Program at Rochester Institute of Technology. Her research, teaching, and administration focus on the intersections of multimodal composition and access; her other interests include writing program administration, writing center studies, and bridging classical and digital rhetorics.

Anicca Cox is Assistant Professor of English at the University of New Mexico, Valencia Campus. Her work centers feminist materialist approaches to institutional change work, community orientations to writing pedagogy, and labor equity. Her scholarship has appeared in several academic journals including *College Composition and Communication, Writing Program Administration,* and the *Journal of Writing Assessment* as well as in several book chapters.

Madeline Crozier is a Ph.D. candidate in English (Rhetoric, Writing & Linguistics) at the University of Tennessee, Knoxville. Her research interests include composition pedagogy, writing pedagogy education, and writing assessment. She has presented at conferences including CCCC, CWPA, and MLA, and her research has appeared in venues such as *Composition Forum* and the *Journal of Business & Technical Communication.*

Cristyn L. Elder is Associate Professor of Rhetoric and Writing at the University of New Mexico. Her research focuses on supporting historically excluded student populations in composition studies and across the disciplines. She is co-editor with Bethany Davila of the collection *Defining, Locating, and Addressing Bullying in the WPA Workplace* (2019) by Utah State University Press. Cristyn has also published in *Across the Disciplines, College Composition and Communication, Composition Forum, Composition Studies, WPA: Writing Program Administration,* and the *Writing Center Journal.* She teaches courses in composition theory, pedagogy, grammars, visual rhetoric, professional editing, and WAC. When she's not on campus, you'll find Cris traveling to far off places (sometimes via her bicycle) or at home with her human and feline family.

Corey Hamilton is Special Lecturer in the Department of Writing and Rhetoric at Oakland University. He has seven years experience teaching first-year composition courses along with technical, professional, and business writing courses, specializing in teaching online. His dissertation focused on the Protestant American megachurch's ability to create an appealing rhetoric that would explain its growth, beyond commonly held myths. Within the classroom, he works to create an appealing rhetoric that edifies, builds up, and thus entices students to learn to learn.

Michelle LaFrance is Associate Professor of English at George Mason University, where she teaches graduate and undergraduate courses in ethnographic and community writing, WAC and Composition pedagogy, ethnography, feminist/cultural materialist and qualitative research methodologies. Her monograph in process is about the hybrid forms of rhetorical belonging at the Historic Congressional Cemetery in DC.

Michelle Miley is Associate Dean in the College of Letters and Science and Associate Professor of English at Montana State University, where she also serves as the writing center director and academic diversity partner. Her articles have appeared in journals such as *Writing Center Journal, WLN: A Journal for Writing Center Scholarship, Praxis.*

Elisabeth L. Miller is Assistant Professor of English and Director of the Writing and Speaking in the Disciplines program at the University of Nevada, Reno. She researches and teaches about disability, health, literacy, and writing in the disciplines. Her book *What It Means to Be Literate: A Disability Materiality Approach to Literacy after Aphasia* is available from University of Pittsburgh Press.

Cindy Mooty is a Special Lecturer in the Department of Writing and Rhetoric at Oakland University with 17 years of experience teaching composition classes. Her doctoral research examined service-learning composition courses at a minority-majority community college—disrupting the normal paradigm of how students should travel across racial borders. Within the classroom, she focuses on establishing the classroom community through student-centered pedagogy, an inquiry-based curriculum, and reflection.

Melissa Nicolas is Professor of English at Washington State University. She studies the rhetoric of health and medicine, disability studies, and writing program administration. Her most recent book, co-edited with Anna Sicari, is *Our Body of Work: Embodied Administration and Teaching.*

Jim Nugent is Professor of Writing and Rhetoric at Oakland University and associate editor of *College English*. His research interests include text technologies, the pedagogy of code, and professional writing. His most recent work, "Written in Homely Discourse: A Case Study of Intellectual and Institutional Identity in Teaching Genres" was co-authored with Megan Schoen, Cindy Mooty, and Lori Ostergaard and appears in *Writing the Classroom: Pedagogical Documents as Rhetorical Genres*, edited by Stephen Neaderhiser (Utah State University Press, 2022).

Lori Ostergaard is Professor of Writing and Rhetoric at Oakland University and editor of *College English*. Lori's scholarship has appeared in a number of journals and edited collections, including *College English*, *Rhetoric Review*, *Composition Studies*, *Composition Forum*, *Studies in the Humanities*, and *Peitho*.

Megan Schoen is Associate Professor of Writing and Rhetoric at Oakland University, where she serves as the director of first-year writing. She currently is an associate editor of *College English*. Her articles have appeared in *Rhetoric Review*, *WPA: Writing Program Administration*, *The WAC Journal*, and *constellations*. She co-edited with Greg Giberson and Christian Weisser the collection *Behind the Curtain of Scholarly Publishing: Editors in Writing Studies* (2022).

Melissa St. Pierre is Assistant Professor of English at Rochester University. She has over ten years of experience teaching first year writing. Her areas of interest include women's rhetoric, communication across generational lines, and writing creative nonfiction. Her classes focus on the idea of community and how the word and definitions change situationally.

Peter Vandenberg is Professor of Writing, Rhetoric, and Discourse and Executive Associate Dean of the College of Liberal Arts and Social Sciences at DePaul University in Chicago. He is the co-editor of three books, including *Keywords in Writing Studies*, and has published and spoken in a broad range of venues across a thirty-year career in rhetoric and composition.

Erin Workman is Assistant Professor of Writing, Rhetoric & Discourse and Director of First-Year Writing at DePaul University. Her research has appeared in *College Composition and Communication*, *The WAC Journal*, the *Journal of Business & Technical Communication*, and *Composition Forum*, as well as in *Approaches to Lifespan Writing Research: Generating an Actionable Coherence*.